Hard Beginning,
Happy Ending

Hard Beginning,
Happy Ending

❧

Marabel Morgan

Illustrations by Marabel Morgan.

ISBN: 1973863278
ISBN 13: 9781973863274

Contents

This story—my story—is written for my daughters, Laura and Michelle.

You gave me great joy during your growing-up years.

My childhood was sad, so during your childhood, I pretended that I was growing up alongside you.

We all had a wonderful time.

And I'm not sad anymore.

Thank You

I WANT TO express my deepest gratitude:

to my dear husband, Charlie, for his unceasing support as I wrote my story;

to Debbie Petersen for continual encouragement and cheer;

to Rachael Stabler for helpful editing;

to John Underwood for literary guidance;

to Norelys Castrillo for artistic expertise and assembling the material;

to Katie Cabanas for invaluable advice.

Other books by Marabel Morgan

The Total Woman
Total Joy
The Total Woman Cookbook
The Electric Woman

Contact Marabel Morgan at
MarabelHappyEnding@gmail.com

Prologue

I GREW UP on Scholl Road in Mansfield, Ohio. Our family never had a car. If I wanted to go anywhere, I walked or took the city bus. I could catch the bus up at the corner of my street on Lexington Avenue. If I was late and saw the bus leaving from that location, I could run through the backyards of our neighborhood and hopefully catch it in time on another street as it headed toward town. The bus was my entrance to the world.

During my grade-school years, my mother had a viselike grip on my life. She decreed that no friends were allowed to come into our house. We didn't celebrate birthdays or holidays. She became a recluse, and I was ordained to be her caretaker. My life revolved around her every wish. Going to school each day was my only escape.

In my senior year, I was selected to be the mistress of ceremonies for our high-school variety show. What a surprise that was for me! I was thrilled but also dismayed because I didn't have a long dress to wear for the performance. Thankfully, one of my friends loaned me her beautiful beige tulle gown—her treasured dress.

On the night of dress rehearsal, I put on the dress and hurried to the bus stop. The neighbors must have wondered as they saw me walking up the street in the long lovely gown. Sitting on the bus, I gathered the skirt on my lap so it wouldn't touch the dirty floor.

I didn't mind riding the bus that night. Being in the show was the greatest event of my life. Nothing else mattered.

After a successful rehearsal, I headed to the bus stop for the long trip home. It was getting late—it was now after eleven. Finally, the bus stopped at Lexington Avenue, and I walked home in the dark, holding the long skirt up from the pavement. I hoped my mother would still be awake. She wouldn't allow me to have a key to my own house. Just the thought of it infuriated me. I was a senior in high school, almost ready to graduate, and my mother treated me like a child.

My house was dark—no outside light on. I knocked on the door, rang the doorbell, and waited. No answer. I knocked again and again. No answer. I pounded on the door over and over, but there was no answer.

I was angry, angrier than I had ever been. I wanted to kick the door in. In my fury, as I pounded, suddenly my fist crashed right through the small glass window in the door. Pieces of broken glass rained down on me.

For a moment, I didn't realize what had happened. When I pulled my hand back through the shattered glass, I saw blood streaming down my arm. Blood—my blood—was spattering onto the beautiful dress.

At that moment, my mother opened the door. Bleary from sleep, she just stood there in the doorway and looked at me, uncomprehending. Frantic, I ran across the yard to my next-door neighbor and pounded on her front door. When she opened the door and saw the blood and my tears, she called her husband, who woke up and drove me to the emergency room.

Somehow, we made it through the night. I don't recall much that happened when I returned home from the hospital, except that I desperately worked to remove the bloodstains from the gown and fluffed up the skirt so it looked presentable.

The next night, the show went on as scheduled.

But in the days that followed, I thought a lot about my shattered-glass episode. That experience was a defining moment in my life. Something changed inside of me. As I had stood there bleeding, I saw clearly that my mother did not care about my pain. She did not care that I was locked out. In fact, she had done it on purpose.

My mother not only had locked me out of the house; she also had locked me out of her heart.

I was beginning to wonder if there was life beyond that cold house on Scholl Road with the broken window.

CHAPTER 1

— ✂ —

Early Angst

I WAS BORN at the end of the Great Depression, and times were bleak. My newly divorced mother went to work in a beauty shop, so my grandmother moved in with us to take care of me.

I never knew my father. He ran off when I was a baby. My cousin told me years later that my father was a "gangster from Chicago." Another cousin said, "No, that's not so—he was a gangster from Detroit!" Whatever the case, I never knew him.

I was raised by my grandmother. I remember watching her roll out homemade noodles on the kitchen table. She let me fling a handful of raw noodles around in the flour and make a mess. I still remember the feeling of the slick oilcloth covering on the kitchen table as I played with my toys.

Grandma was very kind. She let me dunk my doughnut in her coffee, which delighted me. Coffee was forbidden by my mother, so Grandma and I had a deep secret. When she ironed the clothes, she heated her heavy iron on the stove (neither was electric) and then pressed the clothes until the iron cooled down; then she heated it up again. I had a tiny doll ironing board and a toy iron, and she let me stand next to her, ironing side by side.

I stayed close to my grandmother all day long as she sewed and cooked. We colored together in my Bible coloring book. I remember coloring a picture of young David with his slingshot, slaying the big giant, Goliath. She told me stories about her ten children—yes, ten. She told me about one of her sons, Jesse, who had been very sick. The whole family gathered around his bed to comfort him in his last moments. At the end, he sat straight up in bed and cried out, "Oh, Mama! I see a king! A great king!"

And then he died.

That story intrigued me. I couldn't get it out of my mind. I wondered what it could mean.

My only memory of my mother in those early years was when I was four years old. She took me to see Walt Disney's first animated film, *Snow White*. I remember the theater, the balconies on the side, and where we sat. Snow White's adventures were imprinted on my mind that day, especially the moment when she and her Prince Charming rode off into the sunset. I absolutely loved Snow White. She captured my heart.

New Daddy, New Hope

When I was six, my mother remarried—this time to Howard Hawk. I remember the sunny afternoon the first time we met. He was very tall and very kind. He came to our small apartment with a gift for me—a little metal sparkler that sent out flashes of light. I was mesmerized by the shooting sparkles as I ran and played with my new toy.

I followed my new daddy around like a puppy. He seemed delighted to have me tagging after him.

Our expanded family of four—my mother, new daddy, grandma, and I—needed more space, so we moved across town into a nice two-story house on a pretty street just off Lexington Avenue in Mansfield, Ohio. It was exciting to run from room to room in a great-big house. There was a sunroom off the living room, which became my playroom, my very special place.

We had a big backyard with a peony bush of pink blooms, a lilac bush, and daffodils behind the garage, and I loved all of it. There were two apple trees and a Chinese weeping willow tree, and when my cousins came, we climbed the trees and ate green apples and ran and played until dark. For an only child, having my cousins come to visit was the most fun ever! I adored them.

My mother's brothers and sisters lived in the surrounding area. When my aunts, uncles, and cousins came for holiday dinners, my mother outdid herself. Sometimes she made roast beef and Yorkshire pudding. My new daddy was a congenial host who warmly welcomed all his new relatives.

Life was wonderful. My mother fixed my hair in Shirley Temple curls and bought me black patent-leather shoes and a frilly dress—size 6X.

Now I could go to school. And I thrived. One morning, my first-grade teacher, Miss Ward, asked me to stay inside at recess to paint a table. I felt honored. She showed me how to dip the big brush in the paint can and stroke the paint up and down to make a fine finish. I applied that brown paint, feeling like Michelangelo. That simple little assignment sparked my love for painting that I've enjoyed all my life.

I remember one time when my parents had a party. I was sent to bed early, but then I crept down the stairs to peek at the guests. They were laughing at the antics of my daddy as he clowned around. I laughed too as I watched from my secret hiding place. Then I quietly padded back upstairs to bed, content and secure in our happy family.

I was proud of my new daddy. As a young man, he had left school in the Pennsylvania Dutch countryside and traveled for a short time with the Barnum and Bailey Circus as part of a high-flying trapeze act, reminiscent of the song lyrics "He'd fly through the air with the greatest of ease, that daring young man on the flying trapeze." That was my daddy. But that adventure ended when he accidentally flew through the tent and nearly

severed his jugular vein. As they sewed up his neck without anesthesia, he only asked for a cigarette. My hero.

One day, my mother and I took the bus to a house across town where they had new puppies. We bought a little fluffy white puppy and brought him home in a paper bag. I named him Fluffy (of course), and he followed

4

me everywhere. I loved his sparkling black eyes and cold, wet nose. He let me play with his feet—those puffy little pads on the bottom of his paws.

Then, one memorable day, my new daddy told me he wanted to adopt me as his own little girl and give me his name. I was the happiest girl in town. I would be part of his family; he would be my real daddy. He was an industrial policeman at Westinghouse Corporation and carried a billy club, which I could hardly lift, and he was so handsome in his police-man's uniform. He and my beautiful mother made an adorable couple.

While my family was at peace, our country was at war. The United States had been fighting in World War II on two fronts—against the Nazis in Europe and the Japanese in the Pacific. I didn't understand much about the war but sensed the tension when we listened anxiously to the nightly reports on the radio. President Roosevelt rallied the country with his Fireside Chats and was still in office when the Germans surrendered. When he died, Vice President Truman took over and virtually ended the war in 1945 by ordering the dropping of the atomic bomb on two Japanese cities whose names I had never heard before: Hiroshima and Nagasaki.

Suddenly, the fears and apprehensions in the country changed to re-joicing. V-J Day! Victory was celebrated in every town and on every street. Neighbors went outside; children were running and shouting; there were car horns, parades, and picnics; and everyone had a flag to wave. Peace at last! Food rations ended, and for the first time in what seemed like forever, we could buy sugar and Teaberry chewing gum. As our soldiers returned home from war, we sang songs about Johnny marching home again and "Yankee Doodle Dandy."

In that era, many Americans wanted their lives to look like a Norman Rockwell painting—a happy family feasting at a bountiful Thanksgiving dinner table. I had that image in my mind, even as a little girl. That's what I wanted—family, food, and fun!

My friends and I put on stage plays where we sang happy songs with lyrics like "Oh, what a beautiful morning" and "Pack up your troubles in your old kit bag, and smile, smile, smile." We had no shopping malls, televisions, or cell phones; instead, we had paper dolls, coloring books, and the sandbox.

It was 1945, a wonderful year. The United States had won the war and defeated the forces of evil in the world. All was right again. Well, most of the time.

Strange Spirits

I was seven years old when my grandma died at the house one night. Her death was my greatest loss. She was my dearest friend.

One of my mother's sisters came by the house after the funeral, and then, to my great surprise, moved in with us. I know this was my mother's idea, certainly not my daddy's. It was a grave mistake. Why my daddy let her stay with us, I'll never know.

Aunt Lovina was a crazy person. She had a strange, wild look in her eyes. All her siblings said she was nutty as a fruitcake. But there was also an even darker side, very dark. Aunt Lovina was into witchcraft, and she hauled her séance paraphernalia into my playroom for her occult activities. She enticed my mother into holding séances at night to contact the dead. Those evenings when strange people came in to my playroom to hear "voices from the dead" are etched in my memory.

The atmosphere in our house changed dramatically. Now there was an oppressive mood and downright eerie occurrences. Each morning at breakfast, the conversation revolved around reading the tea leaves in my mother's cup. Incense burned in a little container and filled the air with its strange scent. Every move we made (we were told) was regulated by some kind of superstition or omen. In her spare time, my mother visited a fortune-teller.

Aunt Lovina giggled incessantly over nothing and burst into fits of laughter. Then she looked at us looking at her and erupted into peals of laughter again. She whispered constantly to a spirit she called "Dr. White," who, she said, lived on her shoulder. (Yes, her shoulder.)

One day she took me to Isaly's ice-cream store. As we sat at the counter eating our ice cream, she suddenly lapsed into one of her laughing fits. She stared at her shoulder and exclaimed, "Oh, Dr. White! Oh, *no*, Dr. White!" She almost fell off the stool; she was laughing so hard.

Everyone in the shop looked at us with alarm. Her conversation di-

rected at Dr. White increased in volume, and I thought I would die of embarrassment. From then on, I avoided or hid from her as much as possible.

Aunt Lovina drove my daddy crazy. My mother and daddy began fighting over Aunt Lovina and her absurd actions. Finally, my daddy had enough. He put her suitcase and all her stuff on the front porch and told her, "Get out!" She left.

But the damage had been done. Aunt Lovina was gone, but it seemed like the forces of evil had found a haven in our house. Now we had a different kind of war raging in our lives. My parents fought all the time. I could hear them shouting at each other as I cried myself to sleep at night.

One night, I wandered into my mother's bedroom to find her consulting her Ouija board. I heard her ask, "Should I divorce my husband?"

Her hands were on the pointer, and the Ouija board answered, "Y-E-S."

The next morning, she dragged me with her on the bus downtown to the lawyer's office. She started divorce proceedings, but for some reason, the divorce never was finalized. My daddy stayed with us, but my mother moved him out of her bedroom into my little bedroom and moved me into a larger room. She kept the master bedroom for herself.

My mother was angry all the time. One day, I heard yelling outside and peeked out the back door. My mother was screaming at the lady next door. Why? She was our friend, our neighbor. The next day, that neighbor said I was forbidden to ever step foot in her yard—not even to touch a single blade of her grass! Since her yard was next to our driveway, I was afraid I might accidentally touch a blade of her grass, and I wondered, *Then, what will happen?*

Thankfully, I was still allowed to go on the other side of our house to Mrs. Burgener's yard. Her house was like a noncombat zone. Through the years, Mrs. Burgener was a stabilizing force in my life.

Every day, my mother railed against my sweet daddy, accusing him of siding with the neighbors. My mother thought that all the neighbors had wronged her in some way or another, and my daddy made the mistake of interceding on their behalf. That had put him "on their side." He went to work each day and never had time to interact with the neighbors, but that fact didn't matter to her. He became part of the enemy camp.

Next to face my mother's wrath were her siblings. She got mad at the whole gang and announced she was finished with entertaining them. No one was welcome at our house again.

Out of the blue, my mother sold our dining room furniture—the big table and chairs and buffet. Someone came and took it all away while I was at school. The room that had been filled with happy dinners and all my cousins was now just an empty, hollow space. Just another room to walk through. I felt like that room—empty inside.

Jekyll and Hyde

Something drastic had happened to my mother's personality. She had become a different person, nothing like she had been. Instead of her cheerful countenance, she was continually riled up. And she didn't look like my sweet, beautiful mommy. Sometimes her face looked pulled down, in a twisted, scary way.

Then one morning, my daddy came home from work with terrible news. During his night shift, a pickpocket had stolen his wallet and his check for the week. He sat at the kitchen table with his head in his hands. I didn't know what to do or how to comfort him. His check was for fifty-four dollars. It was all he had. His despair frightened me. We were living paycheck to paycheck. What would we do?

Our family was falling apart! I felt lonely and afraid. A few weeks later, my daddy and I were sitting in the living room when my mother burst into the room screaming at me, "Pack your things! We're leaving!"

I had no idea what she meant. She screamed again, "Hurry up! Get your toys!" And she threw a paper bag at me. I put a few of my toys in the bag and looked helplessly at my daddy. The look on his face was very sad. He looked like he was going to cry. I did cry. I was sobbing when my mother grabbed me and pulled me out the front door.

It was all prearranged. My mother's cousin was parked out front to whisk us away to her apartment. We stayed for two days and then came back home until the next big fight. It became the routine, repeated at various times over the year. It solved nothing except to punish my daddy and add further disruption to our embattled lives.

Every day was a crisis. I came home from school one afternoon to find that Aunt Dorothy and Aunt Ruth had come to visit. Whenever the sisters got together, loud talking ensued—yelling at one another, actually. I used to think, *If I had a sister or a brother, I wouldn't yell at them like this. I'd speak nicely. I'd be so happy to have them.*

Well, maybe in a big family, you have to yell in order to be heard. On this particular day, my mother was yelling. Both sisters tried to calm her down. "Delsie, Delsie, be reasonable."

My mother screamed at them and started kicking at them, kicking them in the shins. She actually kicked them both out the back door! I just stood there crying, aghast at the scene, as she screamed, "Don't ever come back!"

And they never did. It broke my heart.

After that incident, my mother became increasingly disturbed and couldn't function in the house. She was convinced that people were look-ing in the windows at her. No one could tell her otherwise. I came home from school one day to find all the blinds were pulled down, and the house was dark. She had gone upstairs to bed. When dinnertime came, she wouldn't come down or get up. Finally, I made a peanut butter sandwich and took it up to her. The next morning, I woke up and got ready for school, but she wouldn't get out of bed.

Day after day, she lay in her bed and shouted instructions for me. She wanted coffee in the morning, so I learned to make coffee, and I took it up to her, careful not to spill a drop. The weeks went by. We quite literally lived on my peanut butter sandwiches. I didn't understand why she wouldn't get up. I thought, *Who is going to wash our clothes?*

She told me to do the wash, and I went down the rickety steps to the dark basement and stood in front of the old Maytag washer. The only way I could reach the top of the washer was to climb up on a box. Somehow, I learned, but with much anxiety. Threading the wet clothes through the wringer was scary—I thought I might get tangled up in the material and go through the wringer too.

My mother's response was critical. "Be careful!" she warned. "Don't get Clorox on your hands—it will eat your fingers off!"

In the summer, I hung the clothes on a line in the backyard that my daddy lowered so I could reach it. In the winter, he rigged a clothesline in the basement. I can't imagine how they ever dried. I don't know how my daddy cleaned his policeman shirts. Maybe he did his own.

The months dragged on. My daddy and I tried to keep the house from falling apart. He kept the fire going in the furnace when the weather turned cold, and my job was to stoke the furnace when he was at work. This was my worst job. I hated shoveling the dirty, black coal. The shovel was bigger than I was, and it was very heavy. The furnace looked like a monster, like the furnace in *Home Alone*, and the flames scared me. But I had to do it, because my mother was cold up in her bedroom.

My daddy should have stood up to her and made her come downstairs, but he never did. It wouldn't have made any difference. She lived in her own world. When he came home at night, he just sat in his chair, overwhelmed. I felt overwhelmed too.

CHAPTER 2

School Rules

EVIDENTLY, MY MOTHER was still on friendly terms with her sister Harriet, because at one point, she shipped me off to Harriet's house in Cleveland. I had never been away from home without my mother. I don't remember any discussion about this decision. Suddenly, I was going to Aunt Harriet's house to stay. I wish I could remember how it all happened.

Aunt Harriet and Uncle Stad lived in a great-big house, but they had no children of their own. Uncle Stad owned the Cuyahoga County Soap Company. I loved to say those words and repeated "Cuyahoga County Soap Company" over and over for my amusement, much to their great consternation, no doubt.

Left to myself, I wandered through the rooms and came upon a gigantic bear rug covering the floor in a far-off family room. For a minute, I thought it was alive. The enormous bear head with black, piercing eyes glared at me. It was lying there on the floor, looking in my direction, its open jaws of carnivorous fangs ready to eat me. That was just too scary. I stayed away from that room.

Outside in the beautiful big yard, I felt safer. There was a hammock strung between two trees, where I could sway in the breeze and look at the sky, but other than that, there was nothing for me to do. Aunt Harriet probably didn't know what to do with me either.

She woke me up one morning and announced, "You get to go to school today! They have room for you. Hurry, get dressed! You have to catch the bus!" Aunt Harriet stood with me at the end of her driveway, and soon a big yellow school bus pulled up in front of us. She helped me climb onto the bus, and then I was alone, bouncing down the aisle, looking for a seat in the midst of all those peering children, holding on, trying to keep my balance—I can feel the angst all over again.

My little neighborhood school back home had only one building, but this school was on a large campus with many buildings. All the rules and instructions and the new experience of changing classes were bewildering.

In the arithmetic class, as it was called, the kids were doing long division, but we hadn't learned that yet at my school. I didn't understand what the teacher was saying. The whole experience was traumatic.

At lunchtime, another challenge presented itself. I had never been in a cafeteria and didn't know what to do. Do I take the food? How do I know how much to pay? Aunt Harriet had given me lunch money, but I was at a loss. I could hear the kids in line whispering behind my back.

When the last bell rang at the end of the day, waves of children running every which way flooded the parking lot. All the buses were lined up, ready to take them home, but I didn't know how to find my bus. I felt adrift in a sea of yellow school buses.

Eventually, I found the right bus. But the whole day was wrought with so much intense apprehension that my memory just shut down. I can't remember any other moment in those weeks in Cleveland. Within a month or two, Aunt Harriet somehow sent me back home. My Cleveland school experience was over.

Many decades later, my cousin told me that when I was sent to Cleveland, she came to stay with my mother. My mother had invited her!

My cousin was only nine years old, one year older than I was. What was my mother's point in all this? My cousin, in remembering those weeks, said, "We had a great time together. We played cards all day. Your mother was so much fun. But she never did get out of bed."

I couldn't believe it. My mother never played cards with me! To hear my cousin tell this story years later was like a punch to the gut.

When I came home from Cleveland, my mother never told me that my cousin had come to stay with her when I was sent away. I ran around the house, calling for Fluffy. My little dog was gone! Where did Fluffy go? My mother wouldn't answer. I didn't know what to do with my heartache.

And I never did learn long division the proper way.

The Peanut Butter Diet

My mother stayed upstairs in bed all through my time in third grade. I felt as if my life stopped the day she went upstairs. I wandered aimlessly from room to room, wondering what I should do.

At school, I sat at my desk and stared out the window, watching the bare branches of the huge trees blowing in the wind. The teacher droned on in the background, but I didn't hear anything she said.

One day, my third-grade teacher sent a note home with me for my mother. Since I could read, I read the note as I walked home. The note read, "Can someone please wash this child's hair?"

I felt very ashamed. I probably looked like a ragamuffin. Did I ever wash my hair? I don't remember. For sure, my beautiful curls were gone. My mother often remarked from her perch on her bed, "Your hair looks like a rat's nest."

We didn't have a shower in our bathroom, but somehow I must have washed my hair. The note from my teacher that day was the beginning of an inferiority complex that I've fought all my life.

I wonder now how I ever got ready for school on time. Getting dressed was such an ordeal. What clothes should I put on? Nothing was hung in my closet; it all lay in piles on my cold bedroom floor. Where were my shoes and my socks? I had to remember to wash them. I have no memory of how I fed my mother or made my lunch or got to school on time.

At one point, my daddy hired a housekeeper to help us. She was mean, slovenly, and lazy, and she sat at the kitchen table drinking coffee. She didn't last long. Then a succession of women came, but I couldn't see any difference when they left. The ironing basket was still piled high with clothes and sheets. The kitchen floor was still sticky, and our house seemed dirtier than before they came. Finally, in disgust, my daddy gave up. No more housekeepers came, leaving me with my 24-7 job.

Our pretty kitchen, which had been the scene of so many happy occasions, now depressed me. There was nothing to eat in the refrigerator—just a half-empty bottle of Mogen David wine and a quart of milk.

We lived on peanut butter sandwiches. We never had a salad or a vegetable. On Christmas Day, my daddy brought home two oranges. Occasionally, on Sundays, he would bring home two links of a big, fat sausage. He covered the sausage with water in a frying pan and let it simmer all afternoon, until it developed a sauce. Then I carried my mother's portion on a tray up to her bedroom. The smell permeated the house, and I could hardly eat it. I despise sausage to this day.

One day in the third grade, I stopped by my friend's house. While she was gathering her books, I watched her mother frying bacon. Her father sat at the breakfast table, laughing with the other children. Sunshine streamed in the bay window, bathing the room with golden light. It was one of those ethereal moments. A lifetime later, I still remember each detail. Imagine—here was a mother and father, cooking breakfast, eating together as a family, and helping my friend get ready for school. What would that be like? The picture of that happy family became my goal in life. Someday, I dreamed, I would duplicate that scene.

Middle School Days

When my mother went upstairs to bed, she had no physical disability, no injury, no sickness. Why would she do that? She stayed in bed through my third-grade year, and then fourth grade, and then through fifth grade, and all through my middle school years. For six long, miserable years, I had to be the "mommy of the house," doing the wash, feeding my mother, tending the fire in the furnace to keep my mother warm.

Every afternoon, when I came home from school, she yelled, "Don't put up the blinds!" That was a given. Then I climbed the stairs and sat in a chair by her bed. No one was ever allowed in our house, not even any children, so my mother was my only companion. Every day, I listened to her rants against the neighbors, the relatives, and my daddy. She had only one story, the

belief that every person was out to get her—and me—and she recited it over and over. "They have all done me wrong," she snarled. "They have all double-crossed me. They're all out to get me. They are all snakes in the grass." She must have repeated those accusations a hundred thousand times. Her story made no sense to me, but once she got started, she couldn't stop until she ran the course. I secretly called it "her recording." She repeated her daily mantra: "Never tell anyone anything about our life. Don't ever trust anyone except me. No one except me will ever help you. I am the only true friend you will ever have." Then she emphasized her number-one rule: "Don't ever let anyone say anything against your mother!" In a bitter voice, she'd send me off to do the chores. "Just you wait until you have children someday. Then you'll know what I had to put up with."

My mother had no friends. The few who tried had ended up on her enemies list. There was no one left but me, and I was on shaky ground, but she needed me to care for her. She called me "headstrong, ungrateful, and hateful." She referred to me as a "jack of all trades and master of none." It is true that I never finished all my chores. She was right.

Being with her day after day, year after year influenced me greatly. She was afraid of everything and everyone, and I grew up filled with fears.

Looking back, I've wondered what my mother did all day in bed. No one can stay bedridden indefinitely without becoming weak. My mother was not weak.

Did she wander around the house when we weren't at home? Our one phone—a landline—was on the desk in the living room. For any contact with the outside world, she would have had to come downstairs. She didn't starve, her hair never grew long, and she never smelled bad. She cared for her own needs—I just never saw her out of bed for six years.

For me, each bleak day merged into the next. I got up, went to school, came home, and ran the house. We never ate dinner together as a family, never took walks together, never had a birthday party. No social life at all.

Even at school, with children all around, I felt lonely. Trudging home through blizzards and snowdrifts sometimes higher than my head, I felt all alone in the world. Alone. Alone.

Winter.

Spring.

Summer.

Fall.

Alone.

Is This All There Is?

The upstairs hall window didn't have a blind, and I could see all the back-yards of the neighborhood from that vantage point. It seemed like I spent a major part of my childhood looking out that window, yearning to go somewhere—anywhere.

One cold morning, I woke up early for school and passed by the hall window. The first snow of the winter had fallen overnight, and in the pre-dawn light, it looked like a blue-gray blanket covering a blue-gray world. The beauty of that misty scene was breathtaking.

I lingered at the window and contemplated life, wondering where I fit into the scheme of things. From far away came the long, mournful cry of a train whistle. Its wail hung on the crisp, frozen air and seemed to wrap its dirge around my heart. Deep down inside, it seemed like I was wailing too.

Why did I feel such deep sadness? Why did the sound of a faraway whistle fill me with a poignant loneliness and despair? Did the neighbors in all those houses feel that same melancholy ache in their hearts too?

I didn't have any answers. It was time to go to school. I pulled myself away from the window to go get dressed.

My mother had warned me never to tell anyone anything about our home situation, so I never did. I did whatever she said to do. She had total control over me. She ruled both my daddy and me from her bed. He never challenged her. I never thought about challenging her. In fact, even as I write this, I feel disloyal. I want to protect her—to give her the benefit of the doubt. She was my mommy.

Young and Restless

The worst part at home was the absolute emptiness of life. With my mother upstairs in bed and my daddy at work, my only purpose was to do the chores.

In my imagination, I became Snow White. She was my escape. Playing make-believe helped ease my boredom and my sadness. Snow White could smile and sing and maintain a positive attitude while she worked. No one ever knew how her heart was breaking or how helpless she felt.

I had no children's books to read, but my daddy had two big books that were propped up in the living room end table. I was eager to read anything, so I picked up the heaviest book, *Ben Hur*. It must have weighed five pounds. I struggled through the first few pages, but it was too advanced for me. I didn't understand it. The other book, *Cross Creek*, had simple ink drawings, which I liked, but that story was complicated too, so I gave up.

Drawing pictures was my relief. Once, in the fourth grade, I absent-mindedly sketched the profile of the boy sitting next to me in class. When he saw the picture at recess, he loved it and said, "I want to buy that!" I sold it to him for a nickel—my first art sale! He showed it to his friends, and they all wanted their portraits drawn. I spent my recess periods drawing profiles. With my newfound money, I bought candy bars and chewing gum. Soon, though, most of the class had been drawn, so my prosperity was short lived.

One day, when my mother sent me to the grocery for bread and peanut butter, I discovered the comic-book rack in the back of the store. I scoured those comic books. My very favorite was Wonder Woman. She became my new hero. I would always love Snow White, but Wonder Woman was the epitome of womanhood! After reading her escapades, I always marched home standing quite a bit taller and ready to fend off any adversary along the way.

My mother didn't allow me to be outside after dark, but one night I sneaked out to the front steps for just a few minutes to look at the stars. Staring in wonder at the starlit sky, I asked myself:

Where is God?
  What is beyond the stars?
    Who am I?
      Why am I here?
        Where am I going?

On Sundays, my mother sometimes allowed me to walk to church about a mile away, and in the summer, I went to daily Vacation Bible School for a week. Singing songs and hearing stories about Jesus calmed me. But we were taught we had to be good to be accepted by Him, and that worried me a lot. I wasn't good. Deep down inside, I was very bad. I had terrible thoughts, murderous thoughts. At times, I hated my mother and wished she would die so I could be free. Then guilt would consume me for having such an evil thought.

One night, I had a vivid dream about Jesus. He seemed to be standing in a clear cubicle, sort of like a glass elevator. (Of course, I had never seen a glass elevator at that point.) Delicate pastel-colored snowflakes floated all around Him, pink and mint and light blue. The colors were exquisite, heavenly. The dream woke me up. I often thought about that beautiful scene.

In the sixth grade, the girls were suddenly into fashion and wore lovely outfits to school. I had two cotton dresses that I wore alternately throughout that long, cold winter. One of the dresses was aqua blue, my favorite color, which made it bearable. Then there were the knee socks—I had to wear them if I didn't want to freeze. Mine came in two colors: ugly green and dark brown. Oh, how I hated them! I felt very ashamed of my clothes and the way I looked. I can't remember how I even got clothes—a coat, boots, and mittens.

My education was a washout; I couldn't concentrate on school. I felt that I was behind the eight ball. I didn't know what that meant, but that phrase described how I felt.

The only happiness in life was my daddy.

CHAPTER 3

Daddy's Girl

My DADDY NEVER said an unkind word about my mother. He must have been brokenhearted about how his life had turned out, but he kept his emotions inside. I'm sure he was sad for me and wanted to give me a little semblance of a normal childhood.

When I turned eleven, he and I took the bus downtown to Montgomery Ward to look at bicycles. There on the lower floor of the department store, two dozen bikes were on display. I was very excited. I looked them all over, and I chose the most beautiful one of all—a shiny blue bike. I whispered, "Daddy, that's the one!"

He seemed as excited as I was. But buying that bike must have come at great sacrifice for him. He put the bike on a layaway plan and paid five dollars down. Each month we took the bus downtown, paid another five dollars, and after many months, we finally brought "Blue Beauty" home—on the bus. That bike was the greatest present I ever received.

I loved my bike, but my mother wasn't happy about it at all. She forbade me from riding out of the yard. I was allowed to ride it only in the grass, never on the street or the sidewalk. So I rode up and down the front yard and then into the backyard, pushing those pedals through the grass. How I longed to ride on pavement.

Riding my bike fueled my spirit of adventure. In my imagination, I could pedal all over the world, if I wanted to—all the way to "Tim Buck Two," wherever that was. Sometimes robbers were chasing me, and sometimes storms were crashing all around me, but I outraced them all.

Then it was back to reality. Back to pacifying my mother, fixing the sandwiches, washing the clothes. And going to school.

Most kids walked home at noon for lunch, but I had to stay at school. I never knew why. Only two other kids in the sixth grade stayed for lunch with me. We played jacks and pick-up-sticks. I felt pangs of jealousy as I saw my friends' lunches—meat sandwiches, with green lettuce leaves peeking out, carrot strips, cookies, and apples. My lunch was always the same: a peanut butter sandwich.

My First Painting

My daddy saw me drawing faces on every piece of paper I could find. He sent away for an art course by mail, which consisted of several books and a charcoal pencil, but the course was too advanced. I didn't have the talent or the discipline to follow through. Thankfully, I kept the books from that course and have referred to them often through the years.

When I was twelve, my daddy surprised me with an oil-painting starter set. That package of beautiful colored tubes of paint, two brushes, and a ten-by-fourteen-inch canvas was like a treasure chest of jewels to me. He also gave me a copy of Winslow Homer's painting *The Herring Net* and suggested, "Why don't you try to copy this?" He set up a card table in our empty dining room, and I laid out my paints on a little palette, feeling like a real artist. I painted the fishermen in rough seas,

and it turned out pretty well. Best of all, my daddy was so proud.

My First Fainting

When I started eighth grade, I observed the elite group of students who ran the place. They walked with a swagger and an attitude. I looked at them with awe. With my confidence level at zero, I dreaded going to school each day. I was especially embarrassed over my clothes and wished I could be invisible.

One morning, in history class, the teacher called on me to stand and read a passage. This was my absolute worst fear. As I stood up, I was trembling. Those old feelings of inadequacy swept over me, strangling my words as I tried to read. My voice squeaked, and my heart pounded. Suddenly, the classroom began to spin around me, and I fainted dead away in the aisle.

When I came to, I was lying on the floor in between the rows. I opened my eyes to see all the kids staring down at me. I could have died of humiliation.

In the cafeteria at lunch, I overheard some girls laughing about me. I truly wanted to die. Fear gripped me after that—fear of others' evaluation and fear of rejection.

That night, I told my daddy what had happened. "I was so ashamed," I sobbed, "and I'm never going back to school." I really meant it.

With great wisdom, he calmly encouraged me, saying, "I know you feel terrible about it. The most important thing to do now is to take a speech class. You will learn how to overcome your fears."

He believed in me. He gave me the confidence to continue. That next year, I signed up for speech and drama, and eventually, with effort and practice, I overcame that fear.

Daddy's Radio

In the evenings, my daddy and I sometimes listened to the radio together. He sat in his chair, and I sat on the floor next to the old Philco radio. We listened to Baby Snooks and Jack Benny and music. My daddy loved music and patted my arm in time to the songs, and I loved that. He had played the tuba in John Philip Sousa's band and had marched down the Champs-Elysees in Paris during the First World War. He had also served in China and told me wild stories how the Chinese tortured the POWs. Strong stuff for a young girl, but he needed to talk it out to someone.

Anytime we were together, my mother was screaming from upstairs, "Turn that radio down!" There was no way she could possibly have heard it; we could hardly hear it. My ear was pressed against the radio because the volume was so low, but she continued to scream over and over: "Turn that radio down!"

It was just my daddy and me, quietly listening to the radio and being chastised. She had us both trapped, and we let her do it. My daddy probably didn't know what to do. Often, he quietly whispered under his breath, "Anything to keep the peace."

It was too late to change our lives. There was no way we could change anything, so we just continued on. Maybe my daddy stuck it out for my sake.

Sex Ed 101

My mother became energized over my sex education. One afternoon, she produced a technical textbook from her bedside table—a book on STDs. She made me look at pictures of deformed babies born to mothers with syphilis. I had to look at all the pictures in the book. The images horrified me and gave me nightmares, but she was relentless. She lay in her bed (still, after five years), propped up on her pillow, delivering her message about men: "And that's why you need to stay away from men. They want only one thing. Avoid any association with boys at school."

But I loved the boys. I loved their bravado, their noise, their action. In high school, I sometimes sneaked out to meet a boy in his car. I always had the unsettling feeling that God was in the back seat, leaning over, watching us, which helped keep me on the straight and narrow. Down in my core, I wanted to be a good girl. If I took drives with boys, I lied to my mother, knowing she would call the police if I told her the truth. I didn't want to drink or carouse; I just wanted some freedom to explore my little world, but she was deathly afraid of letting me out of her sight.

Looking back, I am grateful for my sheltered upbringing. My mother's bizarre sex ed program may have worked. I set a standard for myself that bucked the norm—no premarital sex for me. I determined to remain a virgin until I married.

Daddy's Sick

When I was in the ninth grade, my daddy got sick. He smoked several packs of cigarettes a day and coughed a lot. He looked old and tired and gray. I thought, *He's going to die,* and it chilled my heart.

One day, my daddy went to the doctor instead of work—a first. He returned home on the bus and hung up his coat. He slowly climbed the stairs to his little room and crawled into bed. He did not feel well at all. I went up to see him, and he smiled weakly at me. "Honey," he said, "will you run down to Isaly's and get me a pint of orange sherbet? I think that might make me feel better."

I was a lazy, selfish teenager, and I told him, "I don't want to." And I didn't go, even though Isaly's was only three blocks away.

I could very easily have run to the store and brought it back and given him a moment of joy, but I didn't. It is one of my greatest regrets in life. I can still see the disappointment on his sweet face. If only I could live that day over.

That dear, precious, nonjudgmental man, who had loved me unconditionally through the hard years, had only one request—a pint of orange sherbet.

That night, my ninth-grade class sponsored a school dance, and I was allowed to attend. I remember the night vividly; it is seared in my memory—walking to school, seeing the kids in the gym, and feeling awkward about dancing.

In the midst of the evening, a teacher pulled me off to the side and said, "Your father just died. You need to hurry home!"

The room began turning, a whirling of lights and people and music, a cacophony of pain and noise and my own heartbeat. I could hardly comprehend what the teacher was saying.

I remember the looks of shock on my classmates' faces as they heard the news. Somehow, my legs worked, and I ran out of the gymnasium. I ran through the dark, empty streets, down the many blocks to my house. There was a car parked in the driveway.

I ran into the house, and there was my mother—standing up, downstairs! With her were two other people, a minister and his wife, whom I had never seen before.

I ran upstairs to my daddy's room. He wasn't there. The room was empty.

Oh, the anguish of that night. The sorrow. It was the worst night of my life. I couldn't grasp the fact that he was no longer there. Where was he? What happens to someone when he dies? Surely, he can't stop being. Would I ever see him again? How could I go on without him?

There was no one I could turn to, no one I could ask.

And now, after six years of being in bed, my mother was walking around downstairs. My head was exploding. I couldn't understand what was happening.

My daddy was only fifty-six, and my mother was forty-one. I was fourteen, but I grew up that night. I was no longer a child.

My mother and I went to the funeral. I had never been to a funeral before. Some of my school friends were there, sitting across from us. That's the only part of the service I remember.

Afterward, we went to the cemetery, and as my mother and I stood at the open grave, a bugler played the plaintive notes of Taps. I had never heard Taps before. It tore my heart apart.

Later, the funeral home brought pots of flowers by the house and placed them in our front hallway. The sweet smell of the flowers was nauseating; it was the smell of death. Why did life have to hurt so much?

I mourned for my daddy for a long, long time.

CHAPTER 4

High School

My MOTHER RESUMED her life, such as it was, as if those years in bed had never happened. She never mentioned them, and neither did I. She never mentioned my daddy, and I was afraid to talk about him, so I grieved in silence.

Having her out of bed was almost worse than when she was upstairs. I was a teenager now, and our relationship was contentious. When she repeated her rants over and over to me, I tried to explain that she made no sense. I tried to change the subject, but there was no stopping her.

My sense of inferiority was all-consuming in the tenth grade. I felt I didn't know how to act or talk intelligently; I didn't know proper etiquette or the social graces. The beautiful girls in my class wore wool skirts and sweaters, with ribbons to match in their hair. My pitiful cotton dresses were from a catalog. My mother allowed me to get a job at Tiffin & Toffee House Restaurant after school, and with my earnings, I bought several wool skirts and blouses that I wore day after day.

I loved my job. Several of my friends worked there too. We arrived after school to prep the salads for dinner, waited on the customers until eight thirty, and then cleaned up. The best benefit was the delicious food that we were allowed to sample—dishes like fried chicken and stuffed pork chops! I worked there all through high school.

Then, incredibly, my mother went to work in a reputable beauty shop downtown. She developed a clientele and was lucid at work. It was only at home that she was irrational. I yearned for us to understand each other—to have some fun, but we couldn't even have a meaningful conversation. If I ever gave my point of view, she threatened to call the police "to bring me into line." Since she had called the police on all the relatives and neighbors, I believed her threat.

Still, I loved her. One night, she was sitting on a chair over the heat register to keep warm. My longing for love and physical affection overcame me. I went over and sat on her lap. I put my arms around her and sobbed, "Mommy! Mommy!" I don't remember if she loved me back.

In my loneliness and despair, I often thought about suicide but shoved those thoughts away. More than anything, I wanted to live. I thought, *There has to be more to life than this!*

But I didn't know how to find it.

"Pretend You're Happy"

On Sunday afternoons, my mother allowed me to take the bus to go to the movies. For a couple of hours, I escaped into a world of adventure and love. No matter what the storyline, I cried my eyes out. But it felt good to cry like that.

Being alone in the theater didn't feel lonely. It was comforting, like being in a cocoon. The movies in the 1950s were rather innocent. Most of the love stories had a happy ending. I made up my mind—that's what I wanted, the happily ever after; the fantasy, the fairy tale.

As a child, I had retreated into make-believe. Pretending to be Snow White or Cinderella was easier than facing the drudgery of life. Eventually, I gave up fairy tales for pop songs on the radio and took the lyrics as my theme. Happy songs helped dispel my grief. I wanted to have hope.

Hearing Nat King Cole sing "Pretend" filled me with hope. I felt the words were written especially for me. Here was an answer—pretending to be happy—I could do that! Repeating the words of that song in my mind gave me the courage to go on.

But reality was ever present. The first time I heard Johnny Mathis sing "The Little White Cloud That Cried," I broke down in heaving sobs. Always on the edge of crying, even the word *cry* caused me emotional havoc. Would there ever be a day when that deep sadness would be gone?

A movie, *I'll Cry Tomorrow*, came out the summer after graduation. The story was about a little girl who had an overbearing, controlling mother. The girl grew up, and in order to cope, she decided she wouldn't cry now; she would cry *tomorrow*. Of course, I got lost in the story and cried and cried.

Then I remembered the story line—I can make it through each day without crying, because *I can cry tomorrow*. I thought that was a great way to cope with sorrow. So whenever possible, I stuffed the tears down under the surface.

The Doctor and the Judge

I longed to talk with someone—anyone—about my home situation. My mother had forbidden me to tell anyone anything about our lives. But in desperation, I went to the office of Dr. Heringhaus, my daddy's doctor, and asked to speak with him.

He was a kind man, and he listened as I poured out my story, and then he said, "You are the only one who can put your mother away. You can sign right here." I was shocked, not quite grasping what he was saying, and yet knowing exactly what he meant. I jumped up and ran out of his office. I didn't even dare to let myself think that the doctor was suggesting I have my mother committed.

I wanted to run, but where could I go? I must have threatened that I would leave one day because my mother often said, "If you ever try to leave, I'll call the state militia to bring you back!" There was no way out for me. I was trapped.

When I turned sixteen, I took the bus downtown and walked trembling into the courthouse on the city square. I gathered my courage and asked if I could speak to a judge. I had never seen a judge or even an attorney, and I was quaking in my shoes. A clerk ushered me into a courtroom with heavy velvet draperies and flags, and I stood before the judge. After I told him my story and asked if the militia would bring me back, he sighed.

"When you turn eighteen, honey, run!" he said. "Get out of there! She can't bring you back!"

That kind judge gave me the authority to leave. It was a turning point for me.

Coming Alive

I walked out of that courthouse with hope in my heart. There was an end in sight. I would bide my time, plan my escape, and someday, I would leave and live my life.

But how could I really do that? How could I leave my mother to fend for herself? My plan was scandalous. Disloyal. Disgraceful. Impossible. My mother would never forgive me; that was certain. Still, I stored the plan away in the back of my mind.

In my junior year, a new book, *The Power of Positive Thinking*, swept the ratings. The advertising seemed to call to me: "Have you lost faith and confidence in yourself? Do you want friends and a happy life?"

I bought a copy and absorbed it. Author Norman Vincent Peale suggested that readers repeat phrases such as "I can do all things through Christ who strengthens me." I didn't know what that meant, but I repeated the phrase over and over throughout the day.

The book said, "Smile at people," so I smiled at everybody—and some people smiled back.

To raise funds for homecoming, the junior class decided to sell chrysanthemums to all the students. Timidly, I volunteered to sell these mums. Each mum cost a dollar, which was quite a steep price. Holding my bundle of flowers and wearing a big smile, I approached a student and ran through my memorized sales pitch. He listened, and to my surprise, he bought a mum!

With one sale came a little confidence. That was the beginning. I discovered that talking is fun, especially if you have something to say. I decided to approach everyone I saw. At the end of the day, I had sold more mums than anyone else!

Suddenly, I was visible. The response from my classmates amazed me. A cheery, smiling attitude worked like magic. Some students began hanging around my locker. The yearbook staff invited me to join them as an art contributor.

Suddenly, school days were exciting. My mother was working downtown, so she gave me a little freedom to be with my girlfriends. One friend had a car, and we had harmless adventures, like careening around the city square.

Locked Out

Our senior class was sponsoring a variety show, and wonder of wonders, I was chosen to be the mistress of ceremonies. I was thrilled.

During the rehearsals, the master of ceremonies, a sweet guy, named Ted, taught me the steps of the soft-shoe dance routine that we were to perform. We were soon soft-shoeing all over the stage. I didn't have an appropriate dress to wear, but a friend loaned me her beautiful beige tulle gown.

On the night of dress rehearsal, I put on the gown and floated to the bus stop for the ride to school. I didn't mind riding the bus that night. The fact that I was in the show was the only thing that mattered.

After the rehearsal, I headed home, worrying about how late it was. It was nearly midnight when the bus finally stopped at my street. As I walked down the dark blocks to my house, I wondered if my mother would still be awake. She kept the doors locked tight, and she wouldn't allow me to have a key to my own house.

Just the thought of it deflated my euphoria. Here I was, a senior in high school, and my mother treated me as if I were a child. Every time I thought about it, I wanted to explode. But there was nothing I could do. There was no possible way to reason with her once her mind was made up.

As I walked up the driveway, the house was dark. I tried the front door, and it was locked. My mother was asleep upstairs. Would she even wake up? I knocked and pushed the doorbell. I pounded on the door, but she didn't come. Feeling more frustrated by the minute, I wanted to kick the door in. I had no other recourse than to try to wake her up by my pounding.

The whole scene was insane to me. I was very upset, and in my furious pounding, I rammed my fist through the glass window in the door! For a moment, I didn't realize what had happened. As I pulled my hand back from the shattered glass, I saw blood flowing down my arm. My blood! And it was dripping onto the beige tulle gown.

Just then, my mother opened the door. She stood there in the doorway, bleary from sleep, looking at me, uncomprehending.

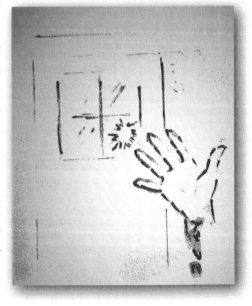

In my panic, I ran across the yard to Mrs. Burgener's house and pounded on her front door. When she opened the door and saw the blood and my tears, she called her husband, who drove me to the emergency room. The scar of stitches on my right hand shows that the glass just missed the artery that runs through the wrist.

Somehow, we made it through the night. Somehow, I got the bloodstains off the gown and fluffed up the skirt to be presentable. Somehow, the next night, Ted and I went through our paces, tripping out the steps to "That Ol' Soft Shoe."

In the days that followed, I thought a lot about the shattered-glass incident. My anger that night had only caused me pain. I decided it was useless to get so mad, to lose control, and I vowed to myself never to get that angry again. With very few exceptions, I have kept that vow.

There was another painful lesson. My mother didn't seem to care that I was locked out or that it had caused me grief. The episode of ramming my hand through the glass revealed a clear picture—my mother had deliberately locked me out of the house and also out of her heart.

But I didn't really see that until much later.

Shattered Scholarship Dreams

In my senior year, we all gathered in the auditorium for the National Honor Society scholarship awards. The names of the scholarship winners were announced in the school assembly, and I heard, "Marabel Hawk receives a scholarship to Ohio University." I was so shocked that I wondered if I had heard the announcement correctly. It was the most momentous event of my life! I was ecstatic. Now I would be able to go to college and maybe make something of myself.

I could hardly wait to tell my mother. She had just come home from work and was in the kitchen when I got home from school. As I rushed in the house shouting my good news, she stopped me in my tracks—literally and figuratively. It was the fury on her face that stopped me cold. She screamed, "You will never go to college! You're not going anywhere! You are going to stay here and take care of me!"

I can still hear those fateful words.

I tried to reason with her: "But you don't understand. This is a scholarship. It's free!" I sobbed and begged her, "Please! Please, let me go!"

There was no use trying to convince her. She immediately launched into her recording (the delusional story of how every relative, neighbor, and man in the world had double-crossed her).

I was stunned. What would I do? What would I tell my teacher? How could I explain that I was not *allowed* to go to college? The whole episode was so painful that I've blocked out all the specifics in my mind. I don't remember the details with my teacher at all.

Losing that scholarship was the keenest disappointment of my life. All hope of freedom was gone. I thought my life was over.

In my mind, I was ruined. There was no way out. The depths of despair, the anguish of my soul overwhelmed me. Alone in my room, I cried, "I'm only seventeen, and my life is finished."

CHAPTER 5

Flying Solo

THAT SUMMER, I turned eighteen. As my high-school friends were preparing for college in the fall, I quietly brought up the subject again with my mother and asked, "Please, can we talk about my going to college?"

That question set off a tirade, but in the end, she said, "No, you can't, but I'll pay for you to go to the beauty college downtown. Then you can work in the beauty shop with me. That's it!"

I was horrified. Working with her was the last thing on earth I wanted to do.

I went to my room and thought it over. Maybe this course of action might make sense. Maybe I wouldn't be trapped forever. If I ever did escape, at least I'd have a means of support. Plus, by taking a cosmetology course, I could get out of the house.

So, in September, I dutifully took the bus downtown to beauty school. The six-month course was interesting, and the customers became my friends. I made up my mind to become the best stylist at the school. With my certificate in hand, I found a job in a nice shop many blocks from my mother's shop, and in due course, I began to save my money.

Amazingly, my mother still functioned during the day with her clients. But at home each night, our family struggles continued. I couldn't use the phone unless she allowed me, and then she parked right next to my elbow. Any date who dared to come to my house had to endure the recitation of her "recording." Sometimes she insisted in joining the party. My date and I sat in the front seat, and my mother climbed in the back. Unbelievable but true.

My mother's paranoia increased. "Enemies" were watching us at every turn, looking in the window, listening to our words, trying to hurt us and steal me away. She was convinced that the Russians—yes, the Russians—were out to get me.

She wrote reams of letters detailing her grievances and sent them to various city officials. She sent pages of bizarre sentences printed in cryptic jargon to the FBI.

I felt like I was going crazy. In extreme moments, I thought of turning on the gas and escaping my misery. I felt like I was locked up in a prison. College was gone. My future was gone. What was the point of going on?

Clean Break Escape

One night in October, after a terrible argument where she repeated her ridiculous "recording" over and over, I couldn't stay any longer. For the sake of my own sanity, I had to leave. But where to go? I had heard the YWCA rented rooms cheaply. You could live at the Y, "a place for girls in crisis," for eight dollars a week.

Very quietly I called a friend to come pick me up and drive me to the Y. She said it would be a while. What if my mother discovered my plan? I stuffed some clothes into a paper bag, grabbed all my money, and waited.

This was the day—the moment—I had dreamed about for years! My one chance to break free, to escape—to live! But now that the moment was here, I was terrified. I had never defied my mother like this. What if she discovered my plan? What would happen when she called to me and I didn't answer? Would she call the police?

What if she heard the car out front and heard me sneaking out the back door? What if she could hear my heart now, pounding out of my body? Anything and everything could go wrong.

At last I heard a car idling out front. I peeked out behind the blind and saw car lights in the dark. This was it. My mother was preoccupied upstairs. I grabbed the bag, opened the door silently, and slipped out. I ran down the driveway, jumped into the car, and cried out to my friend, "Just drive! Hurry!" And we sped away.

My friend didn't even know what I was planning, but it didn't matter. I had made it. We drove across town. I got out of the car and walked into the Y.

There was a sign-in desk in the lobby. I paid my eight dollars to the lady at the desk, and she led me to a tiny room at the end of the hall. My room had a single bed, a desk, a lamp, and a chair.

I hurried to the payphone in the hall and called my mother. She was frantic. "Where *are* you?" she screamed. Then she sobbed, "Your leaving me is going to kill me! I will never forgive you for this!"

Reality was sinking in, and now she was enraged, her voice dripping with venom and bitterness. "You're never going to make it on your own!

And when you're down and out, don't come crawling back to me for help! It's over between us! The bridge is burned!"

And she slammed down the phone.

I was undone, devastated. If I wouldn't do her bidding, it was over— no middle ground. She had been continually at war with everyone except me, and now that I opposed her, she was at war with me too.

Racked with guilt and doubt, I sat in my tiny room and cried, agonizing over my fateful choice. Had I made the right decision? I wanted to be free, yet I still wanted her to love me. My mother was all I had in the world, and when she turned away, I was crushed. I should have known she would never forgive me for leaving her. Now I was truly alone.

Could I make it on my own? I thought I could. I had to try. I wanted to live my own life.

I was nineteen. I was strong. I would make it.

Growing Up Fast

That first night at the Y changed my life. I didn't realize it then, but it did. I wasn't being brave, just desperate.

Life at the Y was a humbling experience. I ate my meals at the lunch counter and occasionally chatted with a fellow traveler—but many of the guests were drifters or worse. Maybe they thought I was a drifter! All kinds of people passed through the Y, but most only stayed for a day or two—temporary lodging for the night. I was there for the duration.

The management tried to present some illusion of social life for the transient boarders. They sponsored checkers tournaments in the game room and dances on Friday nights. Sometimes, locals attended the Y parties.

Over the punch bowl one Friday night, a tall young man and I struck up a conversation. He was the first person who showed any interest in me since I'd left home. I was lonely and vulnerable. We danced for a while, and then he said, "Would you like to see my etchings?"

I said, "I guess so," and then we walked to his apartment. The moment he shut the door, I realized I was in a precarious situation. I felt very tense and wouldn't sit down.

He laughed. "What do you think I'm going to do—ravish you?" he asked. I didn't even know what ravish meant, but it didn't sound good.

We stood there facing each other, and then abruptly he said, "Let's go." He opened the door, we walked out, and he took me back to the Y. I never saw him again. I believe God was protecting me. I was learning how to live on my own.

Silent Night

December was the three-month anniversary of my leaving home. On Christmas Day, I awoke with a sad heart. I thought of my mother. Not that we ever did anything on Christmas; I just missed her.

For dinner that night, I wanted something more special than the lunch counter at the Y. Braving snow flurries, I wandered through the streets of Mansfield looking for a restaurant that was open. I had never felt this cold and this lonely. The thought crossed my mind to call my mother, maybe try to make amends. Maybe Christmas could heal our hearts. But Christmas never soothed any wounds in the past, so I pushed on through the snow.

Finally, on the outskirts of town, I found a Quonset-hut diner with a sign on the door, "Open." The only customer in the diner was a shabby old man, but it was a relief to be inside, away from the cold and wind. I sat down at a table and ordered the Christmas special turkey dinner. I was served a plate with two slices of turkey with canned, cold gravy on top. I took a bite and tried to swallow. It stuck in my throat, as I heard the song on the jukebox, "Joy to the World."

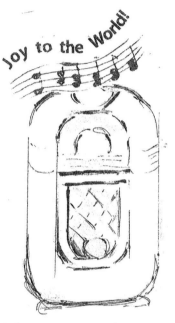

That beautiful Christmas carol brought tears to my eyes. I didn't have any joy. I had no family, no money, no future. I was without God, and without hope, alone in the world.

Trudging back to the Y, I reflected on the day—this day called Christmas. Through the years, at Christmastime, I had always felt like I was looking in on something beautiful, but I wasn't a part of it. What was Christmas all about? I didn't get it. What did that baby in a manger two thousand years ago have to do with me?

I stood under the streetlight and watched the snow come down out of the black, endless sky, and I cried out, "God, are you up there? Do you care...about me?" There was no answer.

I went back to my tiny room and cried myself to sleep on Christmas night.

Bye-Bye, Y

The next morning, I woke up with a new zest for life. I didn't leave home to cry. There was a world to discover, and I had to get moving.

Within a few weeks, I was able to rent a small two-room apartment not far from the beauty shop. I said good-bye to the Y, thanked the manager, and moved into my very own apartment. I had no furniture, just big pillows on the floor, but it was mine. I loved working and dating and living on my own. One young man took me to dinner, and I had my very first taste of steak.

At my friend's wedding, I reconnected with an old friend from high school, and soon we were a steady couple.

Sometimes my paycheck was seventy dollars a week. I was frugal and decided to save my money for college someday. My formula for success—a good job, a great boyfriend, and a lofty goal: college. After four years of hard work, I had saved $900, which paid my way to Ohio State University for one year.

CHAPTER 6

— ✂ —

OSU, Here I Come

OSU Buckeye at Last

GOING TO COLLEGE was a dream come true. I wasn't the least bit anxious. My boyfriend was attending Ohio State, so I had at least one friend as I headed down to Columbus.

I was twenty-two, four years older than those young freshman girls. I moved into a stately old dorm, Mack Hall, and was assigned a room with two other girls. They were already friends but not friendly to me. They pointed me to the bottom bunk bed and never said another word to me as we unpacked our belongings. That didn't bother me. I climbed into bed and went to sleep.

In the middle of that first night at college, I woke up with a bright light shining in my eyes. Startled, I sat up in bed and jammed my face into a protruding nail (spike) sticking out from under the top bunk. It just missed my eye.

I cried out, "What's happening?"

The girl holding the flashlight in my face answered, "The hamster got out of his cage, and we're looking for him."

I was exasperated. Animals weren't allowed in our rooms. I cried out, "What are you doing? Do you think the hamster's in my bed?" How could I live with these girls? It was going to be a very long year.

The next day in the cafeteria line, I met a vivacious girl named Tootie. She was very friendly, so I told her my story about the hamster. She exclaimed, "Oh, you've got to come live with us!" She and her roommate, Sherry, were seniors, and they welcomed me with open arms.

They took me in and introduced me to their friends. I don't remember how I was able to switch rooms, but somehow we did it, and my life took a marvelous turn that day. I was eternally grateful to Tootie and Sherry for their act of kindness and friendship.

What's It All About?

Getting back into the study groove was difficult. College was much harder than high school, and I flunked my first zoology test. I buckled down and made homework my first priority. I studied in the stacks every night, free from all distractions, and made the dean's list.

I realized that here in these hallowed halls was an opportunity to investigate the religions and philosophies of the world. Thinking that maybe they held the answers to my questions, I read volumes, from Bertrand Russell to Zoroaster, but was more confused than ever. Each religion claimed to be true, yet they all contradicted each other. How could truth contradict truth? Buddha and Muhammad and Jesus—which one was right?

My friend Roz lived across the hall. We spent long hours in deep discussion about the meaning of life, but we had no answers. In the midst of all the activities, sometimes an inexplicable sadness would overtake me. The song "Laughing on the Outside, Crying on the Inside" seemed to crush me. It described my feelings exactly.

This melancholy, this depression was always lurking, and I had to fight it off. I put on my best face each morning so that no one knew my inner turmoil.

In my search for truth, I scheduled appointments with campus religious leaders. Each Saturday morning, I planned to meet a different leader to discuss his religious views. I told each one, "I'm searching for the purpose of life. I'm looking for truth, if there is such a thing. I thought you might be able to guide me."

The appointments were disheartening. These ministers were available to meet with students, but none of them had an answer for me. They talked while I listened and took notes. I tried to make sense of it all, but their words seemed like a jumble of rules and platitudes.

One counselor made light of my search and then asked me out.

A priest listened intently as I told him of my earnest search to find meaning. Then he said, "I know what you're asking. In fact, I've had a similar yearning." Then in a quiet voice, he said, "If you ever find what you're looking for, will you come back and tell me?"

That really threw me. If academia and philosophy and religion didn't have satisfying answers, where else could a person look?

From time to time, my friends and I continued to discuss our beliefs—or lack thereof—late into the night. Sometimes the talk centered around Jesus. As I listened, I pictured Jesus as a philosopher in a long white robe, encouraging His followers on a faraway hillside. I didn't understand who He really was.

My emptiness and restlessness drove me to keep on searching.

Beauty School Rewards

One Saturday morning, my roommate watched me cutting my hair and asked, "Why do you cut your own hair?" When I explained I had worked as a beautician, she asked me to cut her hair too. I put a chair in the hall outside our room and began to snip away. Other girls, waking up, noticed the impromptu beauty salon and asked for haircuts too. I cut hair all morning.

Being a licensed beautician, I couldn't charge a fee, so the girls left donations on my dresser. Word spread, and on many Saturday mornings, girls from all over campus lined up and down our hall, waiting their turn in the haircutting chair. Dollar bills piled up on my dresser, which paid for a new sweater or skirt.

I never dreamed there would be such a benefit to cutting hair. In fact, I created instant friends if the haircut turned out well!

Spring Is Sprung

Spring finally arrived. My freshman year at college was coming to a close. My money was almost gone. I would soon be heading back to Mansfield, hopefully to be reinstated at my old job in the beauty shop.

On the college calendar was the long-awaited May Week celebration. This was an annual Ohio State University tradition—a week of contests, games, and fun. The campus became a three-ring circus for one fun-filled week. Racing bicycles flew past fencing matches, sack races, frog races—exhibitions and contests of every description. The festivities ended on Saturday night when the May Queen was crowned in a huge campus gala.

In April, each house and dorm nominated a girl for May Queen. To my utter astonishment, my friends at Mack Hall selected me! Since I had cut many girls' hair over the year, I think they were pleased with me.

Once the candidates were announced, there was a whirlwind of activity. All thirty candidates were invited to appear at a big rally. Each one was introduced and interviewed on stage, in front of thousands of students who were all cheering for their particular choice.

Each contestant had to answer one question. I was asked, "If you had a date with a guy, and he had bad breath, what would you do?"

"Well," I answered, "I would say, 'Oh, I have an awful taste in my mouth. I think I'll have a stick of gum. Would you like one?'" The host laughed, and the crowd applauded. By the end of the evening, I was selected as one of the finalists. I made the first cut.

The finalists then were to prepare for the talent contest two weeks later. Each contestant had to present a song-and-dance routine to perform in every dorm and frat house.

I moaned, "I can't sing or dance."

But the girls on my floor took over. "Don't worry," they said. "We'll take care of everything. You will sing, and we will dance."

They sprang into action. The talented girl across the hall who had grown up in the Catskills summer camps directed the group. One girl wrote the skit, another wrote choreography like *A Chorus Line*. Another worked on costumes.

The dorm was abuzz. Soon the Mack Hall Chorus Line girls were high-stepping in high heels, canes, and top hats.

Everything was set—except the singer. I wasn't (and still am not) a singer.

I had to sing two songs while the girls danced. My friend Roz offered to give me voice lessons in the basement, where no one could hear. We agreed on two songs, "Let a Smile Be Your Umbrella" and "A Fellow Needs a Girl."

Finally, the big day arrived. Late in the afternoon, it was time to go. I put on my borrowed dress. My entourage of dancing girls, my roommates, and the entire third floor headed out across campus. I was scared to death.

At the first frat house, I knocked on the door. We walked into a large room filled with rowdy guys. We were cheered just walking in. That was a good sign.

Then the Mack Hall Chorus Line kicked into action. The guys loved it. That gave me a newfound courage.

We left that house to enthusiastic applause and headed next door. We went to each frat house and dorm, repeating our show almost two dozen times. When we reached my boyfriend's dorm, hundreds of guys were waiting for us, and we brought the house down.

The results of the campus vote were announced the following weekend at an extravagant event starring Louis "Satchmo" Armstrong.

What a night it was. All five finalists on stage. Such excitement, especially meeting Satchmo.

When the grand moment arrived, I was the most surprised girl on campus, when I was crowned the May Queen.

What a wonderful dream, an amazing, astounding turn of events. The girls at Mack Hall had affirmed me and loved me. They would never know what a great gift they had given me.

CHAPTER 7

—— ✂ ——

Mary, Mary

AFTER ONE EXCITING year at college, it was back to Mansfield and the beauty shop. Back to the real world. Back to mundane days of nonstop work. I walked to the shop in rain, snow, or shine and stood on my feet all day, sometimes putting in twelve-hour days.

On Saturday nights, a group of high-school friends often drove up to Lake Erie for Big Band dances at Cedar Point. That was the reward for working all week. Endless days of work and big Saturday night celebrations were typical for my small-town Midwest way of life.

In the beauty shop, I pasted little slogans on my mirror to inspire my customers and myself. Unoriginal phrases like "Keep on keeping on" and "Turn over a new leaf" probably didn't cheer anyone up, but that was all I knew.

In the midst of the gossip at the shop, sometimes the conversations turned philosophical. I told my customers, "I'm looking for purpose, for truth. What do you believe?"

One woman asked me, "Why are you worried about this? You're so young! Go have fun!"

Why *was* I worried about it? I only knew that my questions burned inside of me. That summer, I turned twenty-three. I thought, *If I ever hear truth, surely I will know it, and then I can embrace it.*

But where to look? Were there any answers anywhere?

One morning, the wife of the local butcher brought her young daughter in for a haircut. Soon the mother, Mary Wilging, became my steady customer. She was the most effervescent person I had ever met. I was awed by her enthusiasm and zest for life. When she walked into the shop, she exuded life. She had a certain aura, a peace about her. When she settled into the chair, she would often say, "Oh, I have to tell you what the Lord did for me this week!" The Lord must have hung around her house a lot, because she told me stories about Him all the time.

I had never heard anyone talk like that. She acted like she actually knew the Lord. I was embarrassed, so I turned on my faucets full force so my coworkers wouldn't hear what she was saying.

But Mary intrigued me. I didn't know what made her tick, but whatever it was, I wanted it.

Early one evening when I was working late, she bounced into the shop carrying a tray covered with a tea towel. "I brought you dinner, honey," she said. "Enjoy it! See you later."

I was speechless. My coworkers all stopped and stared. They watched while I lifted the towel to see a dinner of roast beef, mashed potatoes, and a salad. A slice of chocolate cake and a Mason jar of cold milk filled out the tray. It was a most delicious dinner.

I wondered why Mary would do this for me. From time to time, she brought me dinner, placing the tray at my station and flying out to her car.

Each week at her appointment, she talked about the Lord and how He had helped her in a special way.

New Life

I told Mary that I was searching for truth and meaning to life. She told me, "God loves you, and He proved His love by coming to earth to die for you to pay the penalty for all your sins. That's the gospel; it means 'good news.'" She explained that the only way I could be forgiven and go to heaven someday was to thank Jesus for the payment He made for me.

I didn't understand all that, but I knew I had plenty of sin, and I longed to be forgiven. I knew Jesus was the Savior of the world, but Mary explained I needed Him to be my *personal* Savior.

And so I prayed a prayer to Him: "Jesus, I am sorry for all that I've done wrong. Thank you for dying on the cross in my place. I want you to be my Savior."

There was no bolt of lightning or any great emotional experience, but after I said that prayer, I was filled with peace. I had never known peace before. I didn't do anything to get it. Jesus just gave it! It was a gift. I was clean and forgiven.

The next day on the way to work, it seemed to me that the grass looked greener, and the sky looked bluer. I seemed to be brand new. I was looking at the world through new eyes.

In the days that followed, I began to learn more about Jesus. He had put me on a new path. He had given me a new song to sing—not pretending to be happy, but having real peace and joy. I began to understand that I didn't have to search anymore for purpose and meaning.

Jesus said, "I am the way and the truth and the life. No one comes to the Father except through me" (John 14:6). I learned that Jesus is the truth. Now I belonged to Him, and He had a plan for my life—here on earth, and someday in heaven.

I finally realized it's not so important where you've come from; it's where you're going that matters.

New Family

Mary welcomed me into her family. She often picked me up after work and took me home to have dinner with her husband and four beautiful children. To my eyes, this family looked like a beautiful Christmas card—a fairy tale, happiness personified. I'd sit at their kitchen table and wonder if this was really happening. I could hardly believe I could be there, included in their love.

The most beautiful sight to me was Mary's cranberry glass lamp sitting in the kitchen window, framed by ruffled white curtains. The lamp cast a soft rosy glow over the newly fallen snow on the front steps, calling to me, "Come in!"

Her house looked exactly the way a house should look—inviting, light, and bright! Mary loved happy colors like lime green, hot pink, and apricot—very unusual choices for Ohio. When you came in the front door out of a blowing snowstorm, you thought you had just taken a flight to an island paradise!

Mary was all about joy. She taught me to look for joy in little ways— a cardinal singing outside in the snow, or the morning glories climbing up the arbor by the side kitchen door. Cutting up a red pepper, folding clothes, or planning our day—just being alive was cause for joy.

I watched her as she took care of her family, as she entertained, as she brought in lost and lonely people—like me. Mary showed me how to cook a roast, how to bleach my tea towels, and how to welcome and love people. She and her family were the exact opposite of what I had known growing up.

Mary gave me a Bible. It was a treasure to me. I couldn't get enough. I was starving for those words. I had heard the Bible contained great literature, but I hadn't known it contained the words of life. Those words began to change my thinking. Hope was welling up inside me. Perhaps God really *did* have a plan for my life.

I had been programmed to be negative and fearful, but the Bible said we didn't need to fear. God's promises were positive and strong! One of His promises I especially loved was "Call to Me, and I will answer you, and tell you great and unsearchable things you do not know" (Jeremiah 33:3).

Every morning before I walked to work, I sat at my tiny kitchen table and read a small portion of the Scriptures. For the first time, the Bible made sense to me. Mary explained, "Well, now you know the Author of the book, and He is helping you to understand."

Reading about Jesus's life was eye opening. He was so approachable, and all kinds of people followed Him. He was the kind of person you wanted to invite home for dinner. And in fact, He went to dinner with the riffraff and down-and-outers as well as the high and mighty. At weddings, He was the life of the party.

Not everyone agreed with Him, of course, but when He spoke, everyone listened. Jesus said, "Follow me" (Matthew 9:9), and I wanted to. Following Him would be the highest honor of my life.

Choose This Day

I hadn't seen my mother, but through the grapevine, I heard that she got married. I shouldn't have been surprised. She was able to turn on the charm when she wanted to, and with her beauty, she could captivate any unsuspecting soul.

The news was impressive. Her new husband had a fine reputation as the city's fire chief. He had whisked her away to a brand-new home in a lovely neighborhood, and she was no longer working in a beauty shop. Knowing that she was safe helped alleviate my concern.

My world now seemed brand new, like I had come out of the dark into brilliant sunshine. I was filled with deep peace, and I wanted my mother to have that joy and peace too.

The bridge between us hadn't exactly burned all the way down, so I called her. She seemed surprised by my call but allowed me to come over to her new house. Our relationship was strained, but she had softened a little after her marriage. I was able to tell her about my friends and what was happening in my life.

Then I explained my new faith in Jesus, but that part didn't go so well. My mother was very defensive. "I don't need a savior!" she exploded. "I've never done anything wrong!" She was so worked up that I decided to leave.

Whenever I stopped by after that, she started arguing about Jesus. I tried to explain how much God loves us, but she didn't want to hear it.

Eventually she gave me her ultimatum. "You have to choose," she yelled at me. "You can't have Jesus—and me."

I cried, "How can you say that? I love you. But I've been looking for God all my life, and now that I've found Him, I'm going to follow Him forever."

"Then get out!" she shouted. "And don't ever come back!"

She opened her door to me only one time after that.

At the same time, my boyfriend was antagonistic toward Jesus. We argued about Him continually. I couldn't understand it. To me, Jesus was irresistible.

Bewildered and sad, I read Jesus's words: "In this world you will have trouble. But take heart! I have overcome the world" (John 16:33). He also said, "You will know the truth, and the truth will set you free" (John 8:32). That was the longing of my heart—to be free.

CHAPTER 8

— ⚘ —

Florida Beckons

ON A WHIM, I decided to contact my mother's older sister and her husband, who lived in Florida. As a third grader, I had stayed with them during that troubled time in my life. Now, sixteen years later, I yearned for some family connection. Perhaps it was a providential yearning.

I called Aunt Harriet and Uncle Stad, who had left Cleveland and settled in Fort Lauderdale. They invited me down for a little vacation in the land of balmy breezes and turquoise waters.

Aunt Harriet had been the stable one in my mother's family of ten. Maybe she would have some advice for me. She and Uncle Stad wanted to know all that was happening in my life. We basked in the sun together, and I told them about my new faith in Jesus.

During my visit, I read that Billy Graham was speaking in Miami Beach. Aunt Harriet and I drove down to Miami and joined thousands of people at the Miami Beach Convention Center to hear the famous evangelist. It was a glorious evening for me.

After Dr. Graham's message, I met a nice young man who was studying at Miami Bible College. *That is exactly what I want to do,* I thought. *Learn the Bible in a year.* I had to hurry, learn it quickly, to make up for lost time.

That decision to take a year to study the Bible was life changing, but it wasn't easy. Some of my friends thought I had flipped out, and that hurt. In fact, the whole year was laden with heartache. The pain of saying good-bye to my boyfriend, my mother's rejection, and loneliness all weighed on my mind.

Nevertheless, I enrolled at Miami Bible College in the fall. The classes each day outweighed any sadness. I knew this was where I was supposed to be. Learning the Scriptures and the claims of Jesus inspired me. His words of life spoke to me.

The choir director at the college was a lovely woman named Corabel Morgan. I couldn't sing, but I joined the choir just to be close to her. Everybody loved Mrs. Morgan and turned to her for advice.

Unknown to me, she had written to her son, Charlie, at Wheaton College and mentioned she had met a nice girl from Ohio. When Charlie came home for spring break, he was curious.

On a Saturday morning, I was at my new part-time job in a doughnut shop when in walked a handsome man in a dark suit. He bought a doughnut and introduced himself as Charlie Morgan, and we talked for quite a while.

It flustered me a little bit. I didn't know whether to keep on chatting or pretend to rearrange the doughnuts. After all, it was my first hour on the job, and I knew the owner was watching us from the kitchen window. I thought maybe I'd get fired before I even started.

Meanwhile, Charlie seemed content, eating his doughnut and talking. He had just enrolled in law school at the University of Miami. Nearly two hours later, he said he'd better be going and that it was nice talking to me. That was it—he didn't even ask for my telephone number. Life went on.

My college friends and I spent weekends at the University of Miami, talking to students about the purpose of life. We had many rewarding encounters.

The Plot Thickens

When school started in the fall, Charlie called me to ask me for lunch. We went to Dean's Waffle House and sat in a booth across from each other and talked for a long time. He opened up about law school, his dreams, and his seventh-grade Sunday school class. He loved those kids, and I was impressed with his dedication.

Throughout the year, Charlie and I became good friends—not boyfriend/girlfriend, just good friends. I told him about my former boyfriend in Ohio, but that didn't dissuade Charlie. We continued going to football games and playing tennis on the weekends.

In the spring, I got a call from my boyfriend in Ohio. He played shortstop for the Ohio State baseball team, and he said they would be playing Miami in a couple of weeks. Could we get together while he was in town?

What a dilemma. I was thrilled that he was coming, but my times with Charlie were so enjoyable that I didn't want to jeopardize our relationship. Charlie seemed to think my past life in Ohio was a closed chapter. This visit would certainly complicate the situation.

Compounding the problem was transportation. I didn't have a car, but I knew who did.

Charlie had just purchased a new car—a custom-made silver and burgundy Pontiac LeMans with white bucket seats.

At dinner one night, I told him my friend was coming to town. Then I asked hesitantly, "Do you think I could borrow your car for a day to show him around the city?"

Charlie did a double take and repeated, "You want to borrow my car to drive him around town?"

To my utter surprise, he agreed. I don't remember how he got to school.

The time with my boyfriend was well spent. Being with him helped clear my mind. Old memories had been lurking, but when we met, I quickly realized that we were not on the same page. We had different goals and plans for the future. I told him good-bye and returned to Charlie with open arms. Charlie was glad to get both me and his car back.

From that point on, our relationship changed. We found ways to meet almost daily—between classes, at dinner, and on weekends. We could be together for long periods of studying without saying a word, or we could talk for hours. We were true friends.

Charlie was an amazing man. Nothing fazed him. He was kind and confident and steady. I looked at him with new eyes, without any murky memories clouding my view. I was falling in love with Charlie Morgan. The days ahead looked sunny indeed.

Here Comes the Ring

On my twenty-sixth birthday, Charlie treated me to a lovely dinner on Miami Beach. We had a romantic celebration at a waterfront steakhouse, and afterward, we sat in the car and watched the waves roll on shore.

The night was magical. Stars glistened in the misty atmosphere, and a full moon shone down on the ocean. For some reason, Charlie was unusually chatty. He talked about his life, his work, and his plans for the future. Contented, I listened, but with the hypnotic motion of the waves and a full stomach, I fell asleep.

I woke up abruptly when I heard him say, "And that's what I want in a wife." My sweet Charlie, with his analytical mind, had just laid out the qualities he wanted in a wife, and I had missed it!

I was wide awake when he asked me, "Will you be that girl?" He handed me a little velvet jewelry box, and inside was the most beautiful diamond ring. All the superlatives described my state of mind—I was over the moon, flying high. Only one nagging thought marred my ecstasy. I could never admit I had fallen asleep while he listed the qualities he wanted in a wife, but I needed to know—what *were* those qualities?

Here Comes the Bride

We were married in January, in between semesters. I didn't have two nickels to my name. One of my friends loaned me her gown, and another provided the wedding cake. My bridesmaids made their own lavender taffeta dresses, and Charlie's father provided orchid bouquets for the girls to carry.

There never was a happier bride! My heart was bursting with joy over God's plan for our lives—that I could be Mrs. Charles Morgan. I loved my new name and my new husband!

That first year of marriage was blissful. We had few responsibilities. We entertained friends and family, and in my spare moments, I painted the living room walls and tested new recipes for romantic dinners.

In October, we discovered the greatest news: we were going to have a baby! This was the dream of my life coming true.

I spent every waking moment preparing for this baby, while Charlie spent every waking moment planning for law school graduation.

CHAPTER 9

—— ✂ ——

Two Becomes
Three, Four

IN APRIL, JUST before graduation, Charlie received a full scholarship to New York University for a master's degree in tax law.

Our darling baby girl, Laura, was born in early May. We planned to head to New York City in August, to Greenwich Village—our home for the next year. (The beautiful Pontiac LeMans had been replaced by an old station wagon for practical reasons.)

I will never forget that Sunday afternoon in late August when we drove in to Greenwich Village with our stacked suitcases, pots and pans, blankets, heavy coats—and a port-a-crib, in the folded-down backseat. In the midst of bumper-to-bumper traffic and horns honking, Charlie finally found our new home. It was a seventeen-story brick building at 33 Washington Square West. The building was owned by NYU and was used to house the graduate law students.

Charlie drove around and around looking for a parking space—but in NYC, there was no parking. Finally, he double-parked in front of the school and hurried inside. After a few minutes, he came back to the car, crestfallen. "The woman at registration said, 'I'm sorry. Check-in is tomorrow—Monday morning when the school opens.'"

He didn't know what to do. It was now 4:00 p.m. on a hot summer day. We had no place to park our car filled with all our belongings, and no place to lay our tired bodies down.

I was dismayed. I told Charlie, "I have to get out of the car. I'm going to take the baby into the lobby." All three of us went into the building, leaving our car double-parked on the street.

As we entered the lobby, the woman at the registration desk looked up and said, "Oh, what an adorable baby!" Laura smiled and blew bubbles.

Charlie explained, "We just drove here from Miami, and our car is loaded in the street. Do you have any suggestion where we could spend the night?"

The lady kept looking at baby Laura and then said, "Wait just a minute. Let me see if we can get you into your place tonight."

Miracle of miracles. Within the hour, we were in our new apartment seventeen stories high overlooking Sixth Avenue, with a view of the Empire State Building to the north. We were awed at the Lord's blessing.

Our new home had a small living area, with a table and chairs, a bedroom completely filled with the bed, and a tiny kitchen with an icebox big enough for one day's food. Charlie piled his law books and typewriter on a small side table in the corner. We bought a stroller and a crib for Laura and a carpet remnant so she could crawl around on the wooden floor and not get splinters.

Every day after Charlie left for class, I pushed Laura in her stroller down the streets of Greenwich Village to the meat market and grocery for our food for the day. Everywhere we went, people stopped and smiled at our baby. Laura captivated the butcher who gave me little hunks of meat for a dollar. On those days, I made beef stroganoff for dinner.

We lived through the massive power failure of the blackout of 1965, and, yes, there was the occasional shooting in the park across the street, but all in all, it was a lovely existence—just the three of us. The baby kept us laughing. Life was simple and easy.

At the end of the year, we returned home to Miami, with hearts full of warm memories of New York City.

"But, Doctor"

We moved into a little house that needed some love, and I set about decorating the rooms. Like all young couples, we had our joys and sorrows. Our second baby girl was born at seven and a half months, but she came too soon. After a few days, we lost her. When she died, I thought I would never smile again. For weeks after her death, my arms literally ached for my baby. Finally, through the tears, I reaffirmed that God knows best. I tried to adjust back to life as usual, but it took a long time. You can't hurry grief.

During my third pregnancy, the doctor said, "This will be your last. Only three C-sections allowed." I felt all was well, and I was filled with energy.

In my sixth month, we hosted a dinner party in the backyard. That night after the guests had gone, I began having strong labor pains. My doctor roared, "Get out here to the hospital, now!"

My doctor gave me medications to calm the labor pains, but finally he ordered that my hospital bed be tilted up to keep the baby from coming.

Actual bricks were put under the foot of the bed to keep my feet higher than my head. Maybe the doctor thought that up, or maybe it was standard procedure, but there I lay, with the blood rushing to my head. Maybe the baby would settle down now and rest. It seemed to be working. The doctor said, "If you want to keep this baby, just lie there and be patient." Two months later, at the beginning of the eighth month, I went into hard labor. The doctor said, "I'm sorry. We have to do the C-section now!"

When I woke up, I heard the doctor say, "This baby has the same condition as the last one—underdeveloped lungs," and then I faded out. He told Charlie, "Your baby's lungs have collapsed. She isn't going to make it."

The doctor called in a pediatric surgeon, who explained why lung surgery wouldn't work on a premature baby.

"But what can we do to save this baby?" Charlie was desperate. "We're going to lose her like we lost our other baby! Please help us!"

Fortunately, the doctor agreed to emergency lung surgery on a premature baby—the first time it was ever done at Doctors Hospital.

Hours later, the surgeon appeared and told Charlie, "The surgery went well, and now we wait. We hope the lungs can hold." Our baby had tubes and machines holding her together and monitoring her lungs.

But the next day, the doctor appeared in my room and said, "Her lungs have collapsed again, and it looks like she isn't going to make it."

We were brokenhearted. All I could do was cry. Together, we begged the doctor, "Can we try again?"

The doctor explained, "We can't. Her lungs are not developed enough. Again, if she were a full-term baby, it might work."

Charlie pleaded with the doctor. "What have we got to lose? It's our last chance. Could we try one more time?" And the doctor headed back to surgery—for one last attempt before our tiny infant expired.

After that surgery, the doctor said, "The lungs are holding right now. We'll watch her carefully over the next few hours to see if they hold." The hospital staff watched, and everyone we knew prayed. We prayed for a miracle.

The Lord graciously answered our prayers. The lungs held! Days later, the nurse placed that tiny baby in my arms for the first time. I thought my heart would burst with joy. She looked like a little pink rosebud. Michelle, my American beauty rose.

This was the greatest miracle God ever gave me—that He let this little baby girl live.

Family of Four

After we brought our baby home, she lay motionless in her crib for nearly a year. She had a long, hard recovery. Baby Michelle responded to love with smiles, but physically she seemed spent. We were very worried.

Then, at age two, she rebounded. From then on, she was perpetually in motion, climbing, jumping, and running after her big sister.

Laura had a gift for music and began picking out tunes on the piano when she was three. She wanted to be Mommy's little helper, so she and Michelle learned to cook. Since Charlie represented many of the Miami

Dolphins football players, we often hosted the players and their wives after Sunday games in the Orange Bowl. My little girls were a great help to me in entertaining our guests.

Almost every night, Charlie read Bible stories to the girls. He wanted to pour wisdom into their young minds.

Marital Disconnect

Everyone was doing well except me. Somewhere in the midst of those sun-drenched days, I began to unravel inside. I felt that Charlie and I had

drifted apart, and it frightened me. It was my old internal struggle, that frantic feeling that I was left all alone.

Charlie's law practice was thriving. He was involved with clients, day and night, it seemed to me. The truth was, I felt neglected, displaced, and jealous. I lashed out at him, "We don't connect anymore. We're like ships passing in the night. I can't reach you anymore." He just looked at me and shook his head. I rehashed it over and over in my mind. *What can I do? Our communication and romance and fun are gone.*

With our friends, I acted upbeat and pretended all was fine, but inside, I felt helpless and very critical.

In my state of mind, just about everything Charlie did irritated me. One morning, in my frustration, I grabbed one of his legal pads and began to list all the things that bothered me. They were just little things, but they added up—like every night after work, he shed his clothes and books through the house on the way to the bedroom. I followed right behind him, picking everything up.

To Charlie, it was just a game. One phase of the game was sending his socks flying through the air, like a three-point shot that usually landed just shy of the clothes hamper. When he missed, he just laughed. But I was annoyed and didn't like that game.

I knew my husband was a wonderful man, but I saw he had a few rough edges. I thought I could—and should—help him round off those edges. My list excited me. I felt rejuvenated. I thought, *I have a new project—a project to correct Charlie of all his faults!* I could hardly wait for him to come home so we could get started.

That night, I met him at the door and read him the list, but he didn't seem to hear. He brushed right by me and went straight to the TV.

I brought out my list the next day and the next. I kept up my haranguing for a long time. Charlie just tuned me out. For the record, Charlie never changed one thing. But I wasn't discouraged. I thought, *Give me ten more years.*

I'm so ashamed to admit how ignorant and arrogant I was—to think I was pointing out *his* faults! But I couldn't see what I was doing. I was just repeating the pattern I had seen as a child. My mother nagged her husband and me unmercifully, and I longed for the day when I could escape.

As a young wife, I never would have called my relentless instructions nagging; I was only trying to be helpful.

For one thing, I didn't know the definition of nagging. To a man, nagging means saying it more than once. I didn't know that if a man is married to a woman who nags, it's impossible for him to share his innermost thoughts with her. He even begins to think of her as a second mother, so there's no way he's going to feel romantic toward her.

In addition to my nagging, the unresolved issues of my childhood had begun to surface as sarcasm and anger. Charlie was bewildered and asked, "Why do you keep crabbing at me?"

I didn't know why. I had two beautiful daughters and a faithful husband. Why couldn't I be a serene wife and mother? At last I had the family I always wanted. Why was I ruining it?

It's a wonder that Charlie didn't walk out on me. He was concerned about our situation too, but he didn't know what to do about it. For solace, he crawled into his shell in the TV room.

One morning, I read about a weekend marriage workshop coming to our area. When I asked Charlie about attending, amazingly, he said yes. I was surprised. For him to give up his Saturday to listen to a counselor was astonishing.

The marriage workshop was led by Dr. Clyde Narramore, a noted psychologist from Los Angeles. His lectures and case studies were enlightening. He said, "A happy marriage requires a great deal of work and insight."

During the break, I had a short conversation with him and told him a little bit of my background with my mother. He said, "Your mother's actions describe classic symptoms of paranoid schizophrenia. Counseling would be of great benefit to you, to help you address those unresolved conflicts of your childhood. If you don't talk through those issues, they will affect your marriage. But it will take time."

His words startled me. Was the emotional deprivation of my childhood causing my outbursts? I knew I often felt I was running on empty emotionally, especially in times of stress with the children. I sometimes felt like a child myself, longing for my mother. But I tried to shove those feelings down under the surface.

With two little girls underfoot, I didn't have time for counseling. Someday, perhaps. But I knew I needed help, so I headed to the library for a book on marriage. There were only two available—two thick books on theory. I didn't need theory—I needed practical advice. The bookstores weren't any better. In the early seventies, self-help books of any kind were scarce, especially books on marriage.

I didn't know where to turn. One morning, I picked up the Bible and turned to the Proverbs, which were written by King Solomon, the wisest man who ever lived. I hoped I could find some wisdom. I came across these words in chapter 27: "A quarrelsome (nagging) wife is like a continual dripping on a rainy day" (Proverbs 27:15).

The words seemed to leap off the page and glow in neon light. They hit me hard. I saw myself as I really was, and I was horrified. I thought, *Charlie must think of me as water torture!*

In that moment, I had a flash of insight. I saw that I was single-handedly destroying my marriage. I was the one cutting off communication. I was making Charlie's love for me dry up. I saw it, and I wanted to change— immediately. I determined that day to get off his back and get to work on *me.*

I stood in the middle of my living room and said out loud, to no one but myself, "I am going to stop nagging Charlie, even if it kills me! I am going to accept him just as he is and stop trying to change him." I finally understood that I could never change him; I could only change myself. I thought I'd better do it quickly, while there was still time. It was like a covenant had been chiseled in stone. It was done, decided.

My New Project: Change Marabel

That night, I met Charlie at the door and told him, "Honey, I want you to know that I accept you just as you are, and I won't try to change you."

He just looked at me, blinked a couple of times, and went straight to the TV. He didn't know what to think. I realized later that he was very suspicious.

I felt a little rebuffed but determined—determined to give 100 percent to my marriage, whether he responded or not. I didn't *have* to do this. I *wanted* to do it. It was my choice.

Instead of nagging, I would build him up. Each time I felt a nag coming on, I would try to offer a compliment. I made a sign of Dale Carnegie's words: "Don't criticize, condemn, or complain," and I taped it to the refrigerator. Seeing that sign many times a day helped reprogram my negative attitude.

The decision to stop nagging was a major turning point between us. Not that I did it perfectly. Giving up that ingrained habit wasn't easy and is still a daily struggle.

Each morning, I read other proverbs and principles in Scripture that helped me. I tried to apply these principles in my kitchen, living room, and bedroom. I wrote them on my legal pad so I could refer to them daily. I did not want to forget and revert to my old ways. These were life-changing principles. Just simple, common sense. So why did it take me so long to discover this?

Slowly, Charlie began to respond. I could hardly believe what was happening right before my eyes. He came in the door at night, talking! Not to himself, but to me. He seemed happy, he was playful, and we were having fun again. I was ecstatic. I wanted to shout it to the world: "My husband is talking to me again!"

Settling Arguments

I was beginning to see that the best resource for wisdom was that old marriage manual, the Bible! The principles, if I applied them, worked!

I discovered a pearl of wisdom from Scripture that read, "Do not let the sun go down while you are still angry" (Ephesians 4:26). What a revolutionary thought!

Whenever Charlie and I had an argument at night, I felt frustrated. He'd go to sleep the minute his head hit the pillow—out like a light. But I couldn't sleep and lay awake for hours, rehashing our words and feeling sad and lonely.

Now I had a new principle. I couldn't wait for another argument to try it out. We didn't have long to wait. Charlie was upset one night because I had inadvertently thrown out one of his beloved possessions. I said, "It hurts me when we argue, honey. Could we not argue about it now since it's time to go to bed? In the morning, let's talk about it and resolve it then."

He looked surprised. We didn't exactly make up, but we went to bed without wrath. That definitely improved my sleep, and the next morning, we calmly talked it over.

Another day, I read in Scripture, "A gentle answer turns away wrath" (Proverbs 15:1). I had never heard of such a thing. In my experience, if someone yelled angry words, you yelled back—only louder!

That evening, we were invited to a dinner party. This promised to be a lovely event, and I was dressed and ready an hour ahead of time. When Charlie came home late, I met him at the door and said, "Hurry!" He was tired, and the more I pushed, the slower he went. I was beside myself. I followed him into his closet.

He turned around and said, "Look! We'll go when I get ready. And if you keep this up, I'm not going at all."

I knew I had pushed him to the limit. I was mad at him (and mad at me).

When we finally got in the car, the barrier between us nearly suffocated me. I sat close to the door and stared straight ahead. We rode in silence all the way.

At the party, when the hostess opened the door and asked how we were, I said, "Fine, how are you?" Every couple who came in that night said the same thing, and I wondered, *Do you suppose they are all mad at each other too?*

Charlie and I never said a word to each other at the party, and in the car driving home, I felt miserable. How could we ever bridge this gap? Suddenly, I remembered the words I had read that morning. The phrase "A gentle answer turns away wrath" floated through my brain, clear as a bell. I glanced at Charlie's sullen face. Very softly, I said, "I bet you had a hard day today, honey."

He turned and looked at me, and then he said, "You wouldn't believe."

Then he began to talk. His words poured out about the problems of the day and what had happened, but I hardly heard what he said. I was amazed. I thought, *It works! God was right. A gentle answer does turn away wrath!*

What a concept. Those six words made a huge difference in our marriage. It isn't so much *what* I say; it's *how* I say it. I can say almost anything if I say it softly, with respect. This principle works well with everyone, because almost everyone appreciates a soft answer.

That wise sage, King Solomon, once wrote, "Starting a quarrel is like breaching a dam; so drop the matter before a dispute breaks out" (Proverbs 17:14). Since stopping a quarrel is next to impossible, it's better not to let it begin. It is the second angry words that make a quarrel.

In addition to modulating my tone of voice, I needed wisdom with my schedule. My priorities had been out of whack. I didn't know how to say no when people cornered me. I felt obligated to committees and interests out in the world and then had no time and energy left over for my family. So I changed my priorities and called them the "Four Ps."

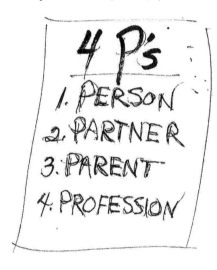

1. First, I am a Person, responsible to God.
2. Since I am married, I am a Partner. My "assignment" is to help my husband.
3. I am a Parent. I had two little ones, who grew into two big ones—with many needs.
4. The public, or my Profession, is fourth on my list. I'm still "out there," eager to help, but they have to wait their turn.

When I keep these priorities in order, I function more efficiently, my family is happy, and there is enough time and energy to go around.

One morning, I stood at the door and enthusiastically waved good-bye to Charlie as he drove away. He drove back, rolled down the window, and said, "What do you want?"

"I don't want anything." I smiled. "I'm just waving good-bye."

He looked a little confused but pleased and drove on.

The next morning, the girls and I stood at the front door and danced the can-can as he drove out of the driveway. The point, of course, was to lighten his load and bring a little playfulness to our day.

Charlie and I were at a tennis match on Key Biscayne one night, and Charlie was acting very amorous, hugging me in front of his friends. This from a man who never even wanted to hold hands in public. One of my friends nearby asked me quietly, "What's happened to Charlie?"

"Nothing's happened to Charlie," I replied. "It's what's happening to me."

I told her what I'd been doing, and she said, "I sure never thought of reading the Bible for marriage tips!"

"Oh, it's chock-full," I told her.

She wanted specifics and asked, "If I get some of my friends together, will you teach us what you've learned?"

"Absolutely!"

CHAPTER 10

————— ✄ —————

"The Total Woman"

IN THAT FIRST class, we discussed things that young wives talk about—family, communication, children, and sex (discreetly, of course). Other classes started, and soon there were groups all over Miami. We called the class "The Total Woman."

In a nutshell, the four lessons from the Total Woman classes were (1) get organized, (2) accept and appreciate your husband, (3) enhance your sex life, and (4) communicate in a way that he can hear you. It was a plan to revive romance, reestablish communication, break down barriers, and put the sizzle back into marriage. The subtitle was "How to Jumpstart a Run-Down Husband." Each class was a lot of fun.

A group of Miami Dolphins football wives attended one of the first classes. Those twelve women went home and did their assignments, and their men puffed up like gladiators! They marched out on the football field and faced the opposition transformed. As a team, the Dolphins won every game that season, including the playoffs and the Super Bowl. That was 1972—the Perfect Season. No team in the NFL had ever done that before—or since.

Some people said it was because their wives were Total Women. I knew it was because Don Shula was such a good coach. Still, it was a fun connection.

It didn't end there. I began to get calls from around the NFL. I was at the sink peeling potatoes one afternoon when the phone rang—some guy from the Dallas Cowboys. He said, "We understand you have this class for the Dolphin wives. It's not fair that only they should have it. We want it too."

Then the Washington Redskins called, and the Minnesota Vikings, and the Green Bay Packers. They all wanted the class. I couldn't go around the country teaching the class. I had two little girls at home to raise. So, some of my friends said, "We'll go teach the course."

Some of my first Total Woman teachers were Miami Dolphins wives, and they were shown great respect as they flew around the NFL, teaching the Total Woman tenets to the wives of other teams. The demand for classes increased, and many of my friends became Total Woman instructors. Some of them traveled the world, teaching the Total Woman Seminar.

A *Miami Herald* reporter showed up at one of my classes and listened to the women telling stories of what had happened in their homes the week before. The next day, the front page of the *Herald* showed a picture of the class with the caption, "What gives Marabel Morgan the chutzpah to tell another woman how to live her life?"

I was mortified. I wasn't telling anyone how to live her life! I wasn't claiming to be an expert on marriage. I was just telling my story. Besides, the principles that turned my life around weren't *my* principles. They were God's! I just happened to stumble upon them. If someone wanted to hear about them, I was happy to oblige.

Friends began asking for copies of the principles, so I wrote them down in a little booklet—the lessons of life as a wife and the examples I had experienced, also adding stories and episodes from the women in the classes.

One day, a book publisher called and asked, "Can you put your notes in book form?" I wondered, *How do you write a real book?*

Personal computers were not around in 1972. All I had was my legal pad, so I put it to use. I taped pages I'd written end to end, down the bedroom hallway floor. It was a perfect solution. I could walk up and down, snipping sentences and paragraphs, and rearranging them in the proper sequence. It was, quite literally, cut and paste.

My little girls thought it was funny that Mommy's papers were all over the floor. When they ran up and down the hall, they sent the pages airborne.

My publisher called often to see how I was coming along. He tried to sound nonchalant, not wanting to push me, yet anxious to get the finished book to press.

But the more I wrote, the more I felt I needed to write. I couldn't seem to finish.

As Charlie left for work one morning, he said in a tight voice, "Finish the book—today! Do it."

I stood there long after his car was out of sight. "It's easy for him to say 'Finish it today,'" I fumed. But I knew he was right. I sat down at the kitchen table and stared into space.

Frustrated and exhausted, I prayed, "Lord, please help me. I don't know how to do this. Please give me the words."

As amazing as it sounds, the words came. My pen was writing, but I didn't seem to know what was coming next. I knew it had to be God helping me. Elated and humbled, I said, "Now the ending, Lord," as if He were standing physically right there by my side. Soon enough, the ending was finished. In shock, I stood up.

If you have ever worked on an overwhelming project that was far beyond your ability and have it finished at last, you know how I felt. Free! A million pounds lifted off my back.

Now to get the manuscript to the editor, to be rid of it at last. I didn't care if it was good, bad, or indifferent; I just wanted it out of my life. Little did I know that it was just the beginning of a new life.

The publisher converted my pages of stories into five thousand printed copies. Charlie and I were afraid the publisher would take a loss, so we bought three hundred copies and put them in the garage.

Phil Donahue heard about the book and invited me to be on his national TV show on a remote at the Wisconsin State Fair. I brought two friends, and we appeared in Green Bay and shared our stories before several thousand women. After the hour program, hundreds of excited women surged forward to the stage. They were very animated—everyone speaking at once.

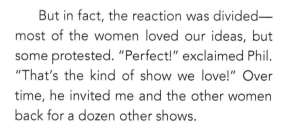

But in fact, the reaction was divided—most of the women loved our ideas, but some protested. "Perfect!" exclaimed Phil. "That's the kind of show we love!" Over time, he invited me and the other women back for a dozen other shows.

It was a tumultuous time in the country. My book came out in October 1973, at the height of the women's liberation movement. The cry of the women's movement was for choices and equal rights. I certainly was in favor of equal pay for women. I believed that men and women were equal in status but different in function. If my choice was to marry and raise a family, how did that adversely affect a person who chose not to marry?

I was amazed that my book created such a firestorm. I was accused of setting the women's liberation movement back a hundred years, although Sally Quinn of the *Washington Post* wrote that I had "left the feminist movement behind."

My book was not intended as an attack on the women's movement, but everywhere we went, we met with opposing reactions. I did understand the pushback. If I had read a book like *The Total Woman* when Charlie and I had not been doing well, I might have been angry—and bitter too. I might have thrown the book in the garbage!

At one point, I was invited to debate women's activist Betty Friedan at Princeton University. The event organizers wanted a fiery argument, with Ms. Friedan defending women's rights and me attacking her. When we discussed the format, the organizers discovered that we were not on opposite poles. After all, I am a woman, and I am for women. My book was a manual that helped me, as a woman, save my marriage.

The Princeton debate was set, and the terms were agreed upon. It would not be a debate but rather a presentation of both positions, after which we would each answer questions from the students. The night before I was to fly to Princeton, the university called to cancel the debate. Betty Friedan had declined. Perhaps it was best that it was canceled.

It is true that the subject of *The Total Woman* caused conflict whenever it was discussed. When the editor of *Time* magazine first suggested *The Total Woman* for the magazine cover, he told me the reaction was visceral. He laughed. "I had high-heel marks all over my chest!" That didn't deter him, though. He said, "If it caused such a violent response, it deserved to be on the cover."

Practicing the Preaching
In the midst of it all, I kept learning and struggling, failing and growing.

Taming my attitude was the tricky part. Just one word spoken sharply changed the whole atmosphere. It took much more energy to soothe feathers and restore the harmony than to just speak kindly in the first place. It was my words that established the mood in our house. How could I ever get over my habit of being negative? When Charlie made a suggestion about anything, I automatically moaned, "Oh, I don't like that" or "No, we can't do that" or "No, that won't work."

What a downer. I decided to answer with a positive response, "Yes! Let's!" He liked that. Actually, I liked it too. Even the girls were being agreeable. It was amazing how certain words could lift their spirits and change their moods.

There were days, though, when I didn't like the idea that my attitude set the atmosphere. I thought, *That's not fair. What about his attitude?* But since it had been working for me, I got myself together before I even got out of bed in the morning. I couldn't be positive day in and day out in my own strength, so I decided first thing to pray. "Jesus, please help me! Help kind words to come out of my mouth. Please help me create a peaceful atmosphere in our house."

Life can become monotonous and dreary. Ho-hum Tuesdays and Wednesdays need new experiences. No matter how grouchy or exhausted the family was when they came in the door, the mood improved if they saw a reason to celebrate.

We started celebrating all sorts of things, *anything*—the cat's birthday, a cool haircut, a new pair of shoes. Celebrate if Daddy comes home early. Celebrate if Daddy comes home.

I realized it didn't take much more time or money to make a celebration, just a little effort on my part—and a candle. You stick the candle in the pizza, and you have an instant celebration. One time I tinted the mashed potatoes pink and put a candle in them. Occasionally, we ate dinner on the floor or *under* the dining room table.

Then, after my daughters went to bed, I moved the celebration into the bedroom.

Romance and Sex

When my two girls were little, our days were filled with playing at the tot lot, heading to the grocery store, and making dinner. I usually collapsed into bed at night, completely worn out.

One day, I turned on a talk show. The guest was the noted sex guru of the day, Dr. David Reuben. He said to the rapt audience of young women, "Most men operate on a forty-eight-hour cycle. That means they need sex that often to keep them on an even keel."

I stood in front of the TV transfixed. I had never heard that before. His jaw-dropping statement knocked me off balance.

I called my sister-in-law with my new information, and she moaned, "I'm exhausted just thinking about it!"

Dr. Reuben also said, "Sex comforts a man and soothes away his frustrations."

As I delved into the subject, I learned that men and women think differently about romance and sex. A woman may give sex in order to get love, and a man may give love in order to get sex. A woman usually wants to make up before she makes love, but a man wants to make love in order to make up.

I also learned that a man has to get past the visual barrier of how a woman looks before he can care how she feels. The same nightie or T-shirt week after week, month after month, can be a little boring, and a man can stand almost anything except boredom.

I had to admit that after six years of marriage, Charlie and I had settled into a rut—the same routine month after month. Talk about boring. I was determined to change all that. I wanted him to be eager to come home each night. It was important for a man to have excitement and high adventure at his own address.

I told myself, "Lighten up. Be a playmate. Make his heart skip a beat when he comes home tonight!" It takes very little to keep Charlie happy—dinner when he comes home, football games or evening activities together, and a little high adventure now and then. This was certainly doable.

To set the scene for romance at night, I needed to pave the way. The first four minutes when he walked through the door set the atmosphere for the evening. Instead of bombarding him with the bad news of the day—"The dryer just broke, the plumber was here, and your cousin is coming for the weekend"—I decided to give him a warm welcome and then let him decompress for a while.

In order to be a red-hot mama, I needed energy. I couldn't be a passionate lover without a plan. So, I wrote on my list: "Take vitamins, plan day, pace self, and set scene for romance." Our bedroom celebration had to be high priority, instead of just an afterthought. Lovely amenities like flowers, candles, and soft music also helped. Charlie responded immediately, and our romance began to blossom.

Feedback to Sex

One day, a radio talk-show host called. "Mrs. Morgan, we've been talking about your book this morning on the show. How about giving an assignment to all the women out there listening? What could the women do right now? Then they can call in to tell us about it. What can you suggest?"

"Well, it's the little things that make a difference in our lives," I said. "Just an encouraging word here and there. So, here's an assignment. Call your husband right now at work, and when he answers, tell him, 'Hurry home tonight, honey. I just crave your body. Bye.'"

The talk-show host laughed and talked about the book. In a few minutes, he said, "Whoa! My switchboard is really lighting up!" Women from all over were calling in to tell how husbands were responding to their phone calls.

Several women said, "My husband was *stunned!*"

One said, "He laughed! For the first time in years!"

An older lady crooned, "Oh my, what a day! I never said anything like that before."

Sometime later, I received a letter from a woman who couldn't get through to the radio show that day. She wrote, "When I called my husband, I told him, 'Hey, big fella—bring your body home early tonight. I've got a craving.'"

There was dead silence on the phone and then a roar of laughter. Her husband's four friends in his office had heard her voice on the speakerphone.

When he came home that night, he told his wife, "I just grinned at them and said, 'Eat your hearts out!'"

I wrote in *The Total Woman* that psychologists say there are only two ingredients needed for a man to absolutely adore his wife: compliments and warm sexual love.

Women from all over the country responded to that news and wrote to tell of their creative experiences.

One letter from a painter's wife caught my attention. "My husband dragged in one night after work, and I realized he needed a quick and sudden dose of both compliments and warm sexual love. After a delicious dinner, we made mad passionate love. And then, I hopped out of bed—and *applauded*!"

Shortly after I received her letter, I was speaking to the wives of a large convention at a big hotel in Memphis. I shared her story with those five hundred women. The next morning, the night clerk reported to the supervisor that all over the hotel all night long—there were sporadic bursts of applause!

Hope Dispenser

The poet Henry David Thoreau wrote that most men lead lives of quiet desperation. How sad is *that*?

In my home, I wanted to banish desperation! I observed that the simplest things lightened the mood at our house—a smile, a pat on the back, a hug. Even a thank-you or a please. And especially, "I'm sorry."

A proverb by King Solomon reads, "An anxious heart weighs a man down, but a kind word cheers him up" (Proverbs 12:25).

There's the answer—a kind word! I know how a person can actually be destroyed by words. But the right words, words of encouragement, can revive a person and turn desperation into *hope*.

As a mother, I felt like a hope dispenser, giving little squirts of hope to my husband, to my girls, to my friends, to everyone who crossed my path—here a squirt, there a squirt, everywhere a squirt, squirt!

The response was contagious among my friends. They wanted to join the League of Hope Dispensers. We were making a difference in how people felt. We began to think we could change the world.

It certainly was working at my house. My family was thriving on encouraging words. The atmosphere at our breakfast table changed, and my husband and my girls walked out the door in the morning with a spring in their step. They usually came back home at night the same way they went out.

Another Scripture put it this way: "Encourage one another daily, as long as it is called Today" (Hebrews 3:13). *Encourage* means "to give courage and hope; to cheer on."

One Sunday afternoon, we all were rooting for the Miami Dolphins in the Orange Bowl. But the Dolphins were losing the game, and the mood in the stadium was very subdued. All of a sudden, Glenn Blackwood, our dear friend, intercepted the football and ran the entire length of the field for a touchdown. The whole stadium, seventy thousand fans strong, erupted in cheers!

We saw that Glenn was still standing in the end zone, staring up into the stands. He was looking up at the section where the Dolphin wives sat. He looked and looked, and finally he saw his wife, Beth, who was jumping up and down, going wild with excitement. When he spotted her, Glenn raised the football, grinned a big grin, and trotted off the field.

In the midst of all those screaming thousands, I saw it very clearly. It was another moment of truth. The whole world can be cheering for a man, but only one person matters—his wife. She is the only one who counts! I finally understood that my husband needs me to be his number-one cheerleader.

And, of course, a cheerleader never quits, regardless of the score.

As a young wife, I didn't realize how my words cheered Charlie when I told him how handsome he looked. I didn't know that when a man looks in the mirror, he sees an eighteen-year-old lifeguard, no matter how old he is! Charlie is now a grandfather, but he still sees that lifeguard in the mirror.

I didn't know that when he combs his hair and straightens his tie in the morning, he says to that image in the mirror, "You tiger, you!" He needs me to see that same tiger. My husband loves his body. He does. It's the only one he has, and he lives in there. He needs me to admire it too. He'll only know if I tell him so.

Since one word of admiration can change the atmosphere in our house, I'm determined to be a cheerleader. It's the easiest way to jump-start a run-down husband.

Wild and Wacky Talk Shows

The Total Woman book evidently struck a nerve. The next year, it appeared on the bestseller lists and became the number-one best-selling hardcover book in the country. We were dumbfounded. It was like a dream, a fluke. Our publisher arranged a book tour to seventeen major cities across the country.

It was a whirlwind tour. The days were filled with radio, TV, and newspaper interviews. For *60 Minutes*, with Morley Safer, I was hooked up to a mic from morning until night for four days throughout San Francisco and Los Angeles. All that for a twenty-minute segment.

On show after show, I told my story. Talk-show hosts fired questions, and the media reacted, mocked, and dissected everything I said. One hostile host in Chicago screamed, "Why won't you just say a four-letter word? Just do it! Give me a four-letter word!" His face was turning purple.

I wanted to stand up and walk off the set. I didn't like him or his attitude, but since it was live TV, I had to finish out the segment. "All right!" I answered. "Here's your word. *Love.* L-o-v-e."

At book signings around the country, women grabbed my hand and thanked me. I said, "No, don't thank me! *You* are the one doing it. You are changing the atmosphere."

During the tour in New York City, I was a guest on *Mid-Day Live*. The topic of the show was "Marriage and Relationships," and there were seven of us on the set. I explained that I chose to give 100 percent to my marriage, with no ulterior motives, no thought of what I would receive in return. This action on my part had turned our marriage around, and I was ecstatic.

Well, the panel jumped all over me. The six other guests shouted at me, and one screamed, "You're a prostitute!" All because I loved my husband and wanted to make him happy. It was an unsettling experience.

The next day, back in Miami, I received a phone call from a psychologist in New York. He had watched the show the day before. "I called to encourage you," he said. "Don't be intimidated by that panel. Your principles work. It takes a very strong person to initiate a cycle of behavior in the home. You've done it. Giving love first is not a weakness; it is a show of strength."

His call invigorated me. Imagine, we women have the power to initiate a cycle of behavior—wherever we go. At school, at work, at home— especially at home.

The news media chased the topic. TV news crews followed us around the house. Letters began arriving from across the United States.

Readers' Feedback

There was a post office box address in the book if anyone wanted to contact us. We actually were surprised when letters began trickling in— sometimes three or four a day.

Charlie usually stopped by the post office when he took the girls to school. He gave them the key to open the box, and they took turns running inside to get the mail.

One morning, Laura came out holding a big stack of letters. From then on, the small box was completely full each day. One day, there was a note inside the box: "Please check with the postmaster at the desk for additional mail." The girls became good friends with the people at the counter. As the mail increased, they bundled and boxed the letters, and the girls carried them out in shopping bags.

We were happy to be hearing from readers, but I was struggling with the thought of answering all those letters. If I didn't answer promptly, people with pressing problems wrote again. One woman said, "I sent a letter several weeks ago and haven't heard from you. Maybe you didn't receive my letter. I am in a desperate situation so I'm writing again. Please answer soon."

One of my friends offered to be my secretary, and I hired her on the spot. Between the two of us, we did our best to respond to the more urgent letters.

The mail increased, filling large post office sorting trays. An entire tray was filled with letters from one day alone. One day, Laura came back to the car and said, "Dad, we've got seven trays of letters today! You have to come in and help me!" It was a paper avalanche.

Each letter represented a family, a mother, a father, and children. I certainly wasn't qualified to give advice, but I could care and encourage.

The letters fell into two main categories: good news and bad news. The good-news letters told funny and tender responses of husbands and children. The bad-news letters asked for help in all kinds of seemingly hopeless situations.

One woman wrote, "I need help. I've been married for one year and unless something changes fast, there won't be a second anniversary."

Another woman lamented, "I've been married thirty-five years. Something's been missing for about thirty."

One wrote, "I just read your book. You sound like a total nut to me. But with a twenty-year marriage that's a total failure, who am I to judge? Quick! Somebody! Anybody! Everybody! Help!"

Even men were writing. "We've been married for forty-two years, and I can't get any cooperation from my wife. Please send all information that you can. Am I too old at seventy-six to dream of a Total Woman?"

Poignant, heartbreaking letters arrived, like the one from Texas: "My little boy said last night, 'Mommy, tomorrow when I get up, you get all my kisses all day.' I feel hope welling up inside, and for the first time, I see my home being repaired. Pray for me—I must run to catch up. My husband and I are separated."

I got encouraging, heartwarming notes like this one from New York: "Mommy, your eyebrows aren't down anymore. You don't yell anymore."

The Total Woman eventually was translated into sixteen languages. It was humbling. I felt it was miraculous. Letters began arriving from all over the world—Europe, Africa, South America, and the islands of the sea.

One letter came from Mr. Nakajima in Japan. He wrote, "I was reading *The Total Woman* on the bullet train traveling from Kyoto to Tokyo, and as I read, the words burned within me." Mr. Nakajima invited me and my whole family to Japan to speak to the employees of MoonBeam, his company. Charlie and I took Laura (Michelle was too young to go), and Laura and I both spoke to the seven thousand MoonBeam salespeople! We had the trip of a lifetime with the wonderful people of Japan.

—— ✂ ——

CHAPTER 11

Raising Children 101

Burden or Blessing

MY FRIEND, DR. Narramore, was a noted child psychologist, who had counseled thousands of children over the years. He told us that a child is either a burden or a blessing.

When I became a mother, I knew next to nothing about raising children, but I desperately wanted my girls to be a blessing. How to do it was the question.

I loved the wonderful promise in Proverbs 22:6, which reads, "Train a child in the way he should go, and when he is old, he will not turn from it."

For me, it was mainly trial and error, raising my children. Thankfully, they were resilient. When children know they are loved, they can develop and flourish even in an imperfect situation. I understood that my job was to teach them what was acceptable in this life and what was not, so they could one day discipline themselves.

At the park one day, my friend who had teenagers, observed my impatience with my little girls who were continually jabbering. She said to me, "If you listen to them when they are little, they will still be talking when they are teens." Her timely advice helped train *me*.

Bedtime became an important time for listening. Those gentle moments just before a child drifts off to sleep is an ideal time for a parent to affirm and encourage. Just the two of us. It became "our time." I heard concerns and stories in the dark that I never would have heard in the light. Our little ritual paid lasting dividends.

Birds and Bees

Recently, a young mother spoke to me about her son, who is in the first grade. "I try to teach my child proper English," she said, "but he comes home from school with gutter talk."

I remember having that same frustration years ago when Laura started first grade. She came home with a whole litany of words on the first day of school. "What does this mean, Mommy?" she asked, going down the list.

"Some kids think it is cute or smart to use bad words," I answered. "Usually the words are about bodily functions. Talking like that is called potty mouth or gutter talk. You know what, honey? I think we are better than that! Why talk about going to the bathroom? I don't want anything yucky to come out of my mouth! We get to choose the words we say; we want to say beautiful words, uplifting words."

Gutter talk is so first grade. But how does a mother neutralize the verbal garbage?

To counteract the onslaught of foul language, we read beautiful children's books; we set a high standard for each of us. We read the Bible to our children and taught them how we should live and speak as followers of Jesus.

I wanted my daughters' lives to be built on the foundation of God's Word. There was no guarantee that they would always choose right, but at least they had a fighting chance. Without the Bible's words of wisdom, a person can hardly withstand the peer pressure.

When Laura was nine and Michelle was five, I was asked to speak to the seventh-grade girls at a church youth group. Since these girls were just a few years older than my girls, I thought that would be an easy assignment.

I arrived at the meeting and saw seventeen beautiful young girls made up like Broadway performers. Their faces—with makeup, mascaraed lashes, and scarlet-pouting lips—all glared at me with narrowed eyes. They weren't even teenagers, yet they had a hard look about them. I felt somewhat intimidated.

I gave my talk about character and setting goals and the value of a good reputation. "It's hard to stand against the pressures of today," I acknowledged. "The peer pressure of drinking, drugs, and sex pushes on us, and no one does it perfectly. That's why we need God's forgiveness. If your past has taken you down another road, the great thing is, with God, you can have a brand-new start."

I encouraged them, "You beautiful girls must decide what kind of character you want to have. You are the one who decides how *you* will live your life. You can have a sterling reputation, but you have to make that decision ahead of time. It's too late when you're pressed up against a hot body in the back seat with the moon over Miami to decide what your character will be!"

After my talk, when the girls were milling around and preparing to leave, suddenly the most aggressive girl was at my elbow. She leaned in close and whispered, "How did you know?"

"What do you mean?" I asked.

"You know," she whispered, "what you said. Being pressed up against a hot body—that was me, last night! How did you know?"

This dear young girl, this child, was caught up in the social scene, where she was pressured to make decisions that could impact the rest of her life. I wondered if she had anyone teaching her how to navigate through these years.

Teenage Turmoil

I spoke over lunch with a friend who had a daughter slightly older than Laura. She told me what to expect over the years ahead. She said, "Just wait till she turns into a teenager—it's murder!"

Charlie and I discussed teen parties, sleepovers, prom parties, and the like. We felt uncomfortable sending our girls into the unknown and preferred that they stick around the house. We redesigned the backyard to allow for teenage parties. We built a putting green, installed a gazebo, and designed the patio around the pool, with a stage for a band. We wanted a house where kids wanted to hang out.

I had been part of a neighborhood carpool, but I didn't like the atmosphere or the language in the car when I picked up. On days when I didn't pick up, my girls had a certain edge when they came into the house and didn't want to talk at all. I finally opted out of the carpool, to the dismay of my neighbors. But I noticed my girls' demeanor changed for the better. I brought along a snack after school, and they opened up and talked to me about their day at school.

On the first day of ninth grade, when I dropped off Laura, she was her usual sweet self. But when I picked her up at three thirty, she was like a different person. No "Hi, Mom," no kisses, just a sneer. When I asked about school, she just growled. Laura's personality had changed in the span of eight hours!

Day after day, it was the same response. I noticed her classmates had the same sullen look. How was I going to manage this teenage angst? The way I spoke drove Laura to distraction. She looked at me with disdain, and our daily confrontations made my heart ache.

The whole year was one conflict after another. I didn't know what to do, but I prayed, "God, please help us!" Weary from the struggle, I made a little sign—"It's always too soon to give up"—and placed it on my desk. Seeing that sign every morning gave me courage to press on.

FCA

One afternoon, when Laura was in the tenth grade, she said, "Mom, we had a guy speak in assembly today from FCA (Fellowship of Christian Athletes). He said anyone can come to their meetings once a week, but they need someplace to meet. I said they could come to our house."

I was so happy that she wanted the kids to come to our house. Of course I agreed. It seemed that Laura had had a change of heart. She was excited to offer our house and my cookies every week for who knows how long. We thought maybe eight to ten kids would come.

That first Monday night, over fifty kids showed up. They pulled up in sports cars, motorcycles, bikes, anything that moved and made their way to the backyard. The leader arrived, a cute guy with a gift of gab and a heart of love. Each week, he brought a guest athlete who gave an inspirational message. I sent Charlie to the store for more supplies. By refreshment time, the brownies and iced tea were ready.

My motto was, if you feed them, they will come. And they came.

I tried to outdo myself each week with food, brownies, ice-cream bars, and fruit on skewers. I memorized their names from the yearbook pictures and spoke to each one by name when they arrived.

Most of the football team showed up, sometimes even a parent or two, to check it all out. The kids met on the patio when the weather was good, and if not, they sat on the floor in the living room. Charlie called it "wall-to-wall puberty."

That FCA group was the best thing that happened to Laura throughout her high school years. She didn't push to go to other parties; she had parties at her own house. All the kids who came each week became an important part of our lives. They were very dear to us. Decades later, we still think of them as family.

Home Fires Burning

The years sped by. Our lives were speeding by, moving fast. I took pride in moving fast, but my acting in haste, on impulse, usually resulted in a botched plan or careless mistake. Some mistakes were perilous and costly. The memory of one misadventure still torments me.

To celebrate the end of a long, hot summer, we planned a big party before the girls headed back to school. On the morning of the party, Charlie left the house early to play golf. Laura and Michelle planned to sleep late, so I hurried to the kitchen to prepare the dinner. Planning a party for my family and friends was exhilarating, and I loved every minute of the preparation. With beautiful wicker baskets hanging from the soffit above the center island cooktop, this was my happy place. Here I cooked and stirred to my heart's content.

I was organized, for once. Talk about having your ducks in a row—in my case, it was pans in a row. All the ingredients were measured; the butter and chocolate squares were in the pans, ready to melt. I turned the burners on low.

Our patio was already set with tables and chairs, and the house was immaculate. I had even washed the trillion little slats on the louvered doors in the kitchen. I felt slightly smug. Bad sign.

With the chocolate mixture melting on the stove, everything was under control. When I glanced out the window, I saw that my red geraniums on the patio looked straggly. On impulse, I grabbed my scissors and a paper bag and headed outside.

At eight thirty in the morning, the sun was already intense, but I was determined to cut and prune each flower. Snipping off the dead leaves, I got lost in the moment. I don't know how many minutes went by. When I finally stood up and glanced toward the house, some movement in the kitchen window caught my eye.

What is that? I wondered. It looked like waving orange shapes dancing in the window. My mind couldn't register what I was seeing.

Suddenly, I realized it was fire! In the kitchen—they were *flames*. The entire cooktop was on fire. I had forgotten about the pans on the stove!

Like slow motion in a dream, like moving through deep water, my legs tried to run across the patio. I opened the kitchen door to see a wall of fire rising from the burning pots of chocolate to the soffit. The orange flames were leaping and crackling, gobbling up the hanging wicker baskets. Black smoke filled the kitchen.

I thought the fire was already beyond my control, but somehow I had to put it out. But how? I pulled dish towels out of the drawer and threw them in the sink. I turned the water on and began to flail the wet towels at the flames. The fire was intense, a four-foot-high wall of flames.

"Oh, God! Help me, help me!" I cried.

I don't know how long I batted those towels at the fire, over and over. Suddenly, unbelievably, the wall of fire went out. The flames were gone. I stood there in disbelief, looking at the smoldering heap on the cooktop. The flames had reached the ceiling light fixture, which now hung down, melted and distorted. How had the flames gone out? All I had were those flimsy little dish towels.

Dense, suffocating black smoke filled the kitchen, and I couldn't see into the living room. I could hardly breathe. I thought, *Open the doors. Don't breathe this smoke.*

At that moment, Laura and Michelle, half asleep, emerged through the thick smoke into the kitchen, coughing and yelling, "Mom! Mom! What's happened?" My beautiful daughters had never looked so wonderful to me. All I could do was hold them and sob.

In shock, the three of us stood there, looking at my calamity—at what I had done. My snow-white kitchen looked like a bombed-out mine. My mind raced—what if I hadn't seen the fire? What if I had gone over to the other flowerbed? What if the fire had taken over the kitchen and spread through the living room? There would have been no way to wake up my girls on the other side of the house to warn them.

I was distraught. What a fool I had been to put pans on the stove and then go outside. God had saved me. I thanked Him again and again. To me, this was an absolute miracle. There was no other answer.

Somehow, the party went on as planned that night. Somehow, there was food on the table. Everyone who came in the front door asked, "Hey, what happened? Did you try to burn the house down?" The odor of smoke permeated every square inch of our house.

I wandered among my friends that night in a daze, shocked to the core, but oh, so grateful in my soul.

All the draperies and upholstery were ruined, all the sofas and furnishings had to be replaced, all the rooms repainted. But of course, none of that mattered. Our family was safe. God had protected us and given me another chance. My Savior had saved me again from a stupid blunder.

Every day of my life, I go into that kitchen, and many times, I have relived those terrible moments. It was the dumbest thing I have ever done. But God did a great miracle for me. I am the most grateful person alive.

My Girls' Goals

Compared with my upbringing, my children have exceeded my wildest dreams.

It all began for Michelle in the fifth grade. After school one afternoon, she led me by the hand into the library. "You have to see this!" she exuded. She opened a travel book to a beautiful photo of the Himalayas. "I want to climb these mountains, Mom!"

From that day on, she aimed for the sky. Charlie and I would smile and say, "Who is this child?" But Michelle had her dream, and finally, at age twenty-three, she flew to Kathmandu, Nepal. There was no deterring her.

She said, "Mom, I *must* do it. I can't get married or do anything until I've done this."

Alone in Kathmandu, she teamed up with two other girls from Boston, and along with six Sherpas, they climbed on the Annapurna Range to fifteen thousand feet. Pitching their tents on the snow-covered mountains, they trekked for eight glorious days. Michelle was deliriously happy as she remembered, "It was the coldest I've ever been in my entire life!"

Michelle pursued communications and languages, with her goal of seeing the world. She is now married with three children and travels the world at every opportunity.

Laura got married in law school, became an attorney, and mother of three. She fulfilled her lifelong dream of practicing law with her father. And Charlie can't wait to get to work each morning to be with his firstborn.

CHAPTER 12

— ⚬ —

Mommy Dearest

THROUGH THE YEARS, at the most unexpected times, waves of longing for my mother threatened to undo me. Each time, I told myself, *Don't do this to yourself. You know she doesn't want you.*

I remembered the one and only time she had relented and opened the door to me. Charlie and I had been vacationing in the Midwest with Laura, who was then four years old. I asked Charlie if we could drive through Mansfield, to see if we could contact my mother, so she could see her little granddaughter. We drove to my mother's house and, amazingly, she allowed us to come inside.

But within ten minutes, she had launched into her old "recording." Then she confronted me with her ultimatum—it was either Charlie or her. I couldn't have both. She said, "Make your decision now, and that's it!"

Charlie very lovingly tried to explain that we longed to have her be part of our family. He had never encountered such a totally irrational person before and didn't know what to do. In spite of all the hatred pouring out of my mother, I sat on the sofa, strangely detached. I had lived this scene growing up, but now I felt no emotion at all. My mother's third husband, the fire chief, sat silently in his chair.

Charlie's face turned red. Beads of perspiration shone on his forehead, and I knew it was time to leave. Little Laura stared at her grandmother, but never once did my mother even glance at her. It was futile. We left.

Over the years, I kept hoping that one day we would be reconciled. Sometimes in the middle of raising our girls or while teaching Total Woman classes, that longing to see my mother would overwhelm me again. Each time, I told myself, *Forget her. She doesn't want you! Accept it!* I couldn't seem to do it.

Against all reason and the advice of friends, I told Charlie, "I have to try again." One weekend, I flew back to Columbus, drove to Mansfield, and arrived at my mother's house. I knocked and knocked at the door and then walked around to the back door and called out, "Mommy! Mommy!"

Here I was, a grown woman, with a wonderful life, begging one more time to see my mother. But she never opened the door.

Another time, I called a cousin to say I wanted to come to Ohio and hoped to see her. She said, "Listen, I'd love to see you, but I hear your mother is on the warpath. She's dangerous. We don't know what she might do. I hate to advise you not to come, but I don't think you should."

I wondered what she could possibly do, hunkered down as a hermit, but there was no point in putting any of us in danger. I decided not to go back. I shoved the longing down inside until it pushed up again.

Even though I knew we could never have a normal relationship, I still yearned to see her. After many more years had gone by, I wanted to make one final attempt. Maybe the years had softened her heart.

I flew to Ohio one last time. I had such high hopes. I even enjoyed the sixty-mile trip driving from Columbus to Mansfield, watching the countryside flying by. Triangle-shaped mauve and beige clouds in rows across the sky looked like a Navajo blanket. The sky looked comforting. If I could just see her—just tell her I was sorry, that I loved her. That sounds pathetic, I know, but it was what I hoped for.

By the time I got to Mansfield, the sky had turned to a colorless gray. Somehow, I found the number of the neighbor across the street from my mother. I tried to explain the situation on the phone. "My mother lives across the street from you. We've been estranged for years, but I wanted to try to see her. I thought perhaps you might be willing to help me. I am right down the street."

There was silence on the line, but I continued on. "My plan is to park in your driveway, and if you could lure my mother out of the house, I would walk by, and maybe she would be willing to speak with me. I know this sounds so weird. But what do you think?"

It was very awkward, very humiliating. The neighbor hesitated a long time, and finally she said, "Well, I know your mother. She likes my little girl. I guess I could try it."

"Oh, thank you," I cried. "I'll be there in just a few minutes." I didn't want to waste any time, for fear she would change her mind.

As I pulled into her driveway, the young mother came out holding her baby girl, who looked adorable in her little hood and jacket. They both stared at me through the car window. "I'll try to get her to come outside," she said.

Sitting in the car, watching my mother's front door in my rearview mirror, felt surreal. I felt like a little child myself. I wanted to run across the street and cry, "Mommy! Mommy!"

The cold October wind rocked the car slightly. Just then I saw her front door open. I saw a hand, nothing more. The neighbor went inside, and the front door shut. *Remarkable!* I thought. *My mother must really like her!*

Minutes passed. The door opened again, and the neighbor and baby came out, but my mother wasn't with them. The door closed behind them.

They reached my car, and the young mother said quickly, "She doesn't want to see you. I told her you were in my driveway, and she said, 'That's over. It was over long ago. I don't want to see her.' Please, could you leave now? We have a nice relationship, and I don't want to alienate her."

My hands were shaking. "Of course," I said. "Thank you so much for trying. And thank you for being kind to my mother." I pulled out of the driveway and looked one last time at my mother's house. Was she watching behind her closed blinds? Did she care at all? Was she crying too?

At the end of the street, I stopped by the curb and cried hard. "Why, Lord, why? Surely you want families to be restored. You could have worked it out."

Words of Scripture flashed through my mind: "Though my father and mother forsake me, the Lord will receive me" (Psalm 27:10).

Then I remembered another word of love: "Can a mother forget the baby at her breast, and have no compassion on the child she has borne? Though she may forget, I will not forget you! See, I have engraved you on the palms of my hands…" (Isaiah 49:15–16).

God's words soothe and comfort. They are enough. He is enough.

The gray, overcast sky pressed down on my sorrowful heart as I drove away. "It's over," I repeated to myself. "It was over long ago. So, that's it. You did what you could. That's all anyone can do. Now turn the corner, once for all, and get on with your life."

Still, I berated myself. Why did I think she would be different this time? Why couldn't I see how foolish I had been? Why was that pull to her so intense?

But at last I did see. I knew there would never be a reconciliation.

My Father the Gangster

I got a call one day from a long-lost cousin in Ohio. She and several other cousins were coming to Florida and invited me to meet them. I hadn't seen most of them since I was a little girl.

For several hours, over iced tea and cookies in a hotel lobby, they shared stories about their lives. Looking at the semicircle of women, I thought this was my one chance to go back in time, so I said brightly, "My childhood is all kind of blurry in my mind. I'd love to hear any details you might have heard from your parents. You know that my father left when I was a baby, so I don't remember him. The only thing my mother ever said about him was that he was a salesman and an alcoholic." I paused. "Did your folks ever say anything about him that you can tell me?"

They all looked at each other. There was a long moment of silence. Then my favorite cousin said, "Well, my mother always told us that your father...was a...gangster. From Chicago." My mouth must have fallen open. I was speechless.

Then another cousin spoke up. "Oh, really? No, I heard he was a gangster from Detroit."

I shouted, "What? Are you kidding?"

They were talking eagerly now. One said, "Your mother had a miserable divorce from your father."

One of the women whom I didn't know said, "When your mother was in high school, she was molested. Everybody knew about it. One of her teachers often took her out of class down to the basement. Then he'd bring her back to class after a half hour. My mother was in class with her. Your mother sometimes cried, and sometimes she laughed hysterically after being with that man."

My mind was spinning. These women were nodding as if this story was common knowledge. I could hardly listen to this without crying.

My poor mother. Who knows what heartache and abuse she had endured? If she had experienced sexual assault again and again as a teenager, no wonder she was so hung up on men.

The conversation continued on, but I couldn't take any more shocking news. I had heard enough. I told them as graciously as I could, "It's been great seeing you all. It's time for me to head home."

Their words kept repeating in my mind—"Your mother was molested. Gangster from Chicago! No, I heard it was Detroit!" These people knew more about my life than I did. My own life was a mystery.

I told Charlie my news. Being the curious lawyer that he is, he immediately went online to search for my father's name. His search led him to Chicago and then to Oregon. After running down some rabbit trails, he eventually reached a man who said he was the son of my father—my half-brother.

Charlie told him, "I'm trying to find this gentleman. I'm married to his daughter Marabel from Mansfield, Ohio." Then he explained, "I'm not looking for anything, but my wife would love to meet her father after all these years."

There was a moment of silence on the line. Charlie could sense this came as a great surprise; the man didn't quite know how to respond. Finally, he said in an ominous tone, "I'd suggest you drop your search. Do not continue on. Good-bye."

That was enough for me. The mystery continues, but I'm no longer interested.

Why, Mommy?

Both girls were away at school, pursuing their education—Laura to law school in Gainesville and Michelle to Wheaton College outside Chicago. We missed our girls, but we couldn't be sad, because they were so happy.

Now Charlie and I were free—the empty-nest syndrome. We could do whatever we wanted to do and go wherever we wanted to go. My dream was to travel to far-flung places like Lake Como and the Fiji Islands.

A month into our new freedom, I was diagnosed with cancer. The news rocked me. The cancer had metastasized into my lymph nodes. In 1987, I thought that was a death sentence. I cried and prayed, but mostly I just wandered from room to room in utter disbelief.

One of my dear friends had an aggressive form of cancer. We grieved together. We talked about living and dying. We weren't afraid to die. Jesus had taken care of that. We would go to be with Him. But we wanted to live now and be with our families.

So, this was my new chapter. I did all the medical things I was advised to do, of course. You plan and pray and go through the treatment. And then you wait and try to pick up the pieces of your life and go through the motions of each day.

I tried to be upbeat, but it was the aftermath, the emotional roller coaster, that got me. I felt that I was slipping into depression. Actually, I didn't slip; I fell headlong into depression. It was chasing me, and I was helpless to stop it.

Through the years, that old feeling of loneliness, feeling forsaken, occasionally would reappear and unnerve me. It followed me. I could picture it lurking in the background, crouching behind me, lying in ambush on the back porch, ready to pounce.

Most of the time, by sheer will, I could hold it at bay.

But after the shock of my cancer diagnosis, deep melancholy came down over me. It covered me like a wet blanket, suffocating me. Down deep inside, I could feel despair rising up, bubbling up, threatening to choke me, and I couldn't hold it back. I scolded myself. *Get a grip. You're going to be all right. Your family is here. It won't help now if you fall apart.*

No matter how hard I tried to convince myself, the despair and the fear of it kept coming. Coming in waves, relentlessly, it finally caught me, and I collapsed under it. One morning, I sobbed to Charlie, "Help me! I can't do it anymore, Charlie! I need help! I can't go on!"

We called Dr. Narramore, who recommended a Christian counselor on the west coast of Florida. He agreed to see me every day for one week. I drove across the state, through the Everglades, desperate to get there and find some relief.

My counselor and I never did talk about the cancer. It was the past that we discussed—all those issues of my childhood that were bubbling up. The shock of having cancer had triggered their release.

I had read that children who grow up in severely dysfunctional families often don't show the effects until adulthood, usually between thirty-five and fifty. I was fifty years old. All those years of unresolved anger and repressed hostilities had shown up, right on schedule.

I thought I had dealt with my childhood. I had been over that ground many times and thought I had been healed of my past. But I learned that healing comes in stages, not all at once. Grief and anger and hurt come off in layers, one at a time. Like layers on an onion, and always with tears.

When I told my counselor my story, I said, "I feel so guilty talking about my mother. Everything about our family was secret. I was forbidden to ever tell anyone anything about our lives. She told me to defend her and stand up for her, and now I feel like a traitor betraying her."

My counselor explained that in counseling, we are not blaming anyone, but we are examining the past for insight, to find clues that cause codependent behavior. Not to blame, but to gain insight. Those were comforting words.

After I poured out my sorrow, the counselor helped me understand some of the dynamics of my childhood and why I continued to struggle, even as an adult. "Growing up in your bizarre dysfunctional family, you were deprived of the basic essentials: love, safety...even social skills, and education. Your mother's involvement in the occult and her abdication of her role as mother were devastating to an eight-year-old child. For her to go to bed for six years and expect you to be the mother of the house was criminal."

The counselor helped me understand the role reversal in my family—when my mother abandoned her role, she became the child. I had to become the parent and take care of her, but it was too much for me. My whole life was upside down. I felt adrift, without an anchor.

I explained that I could never challenge her. Her psychotic tendencies made her all powerful in my eyes. Her grandiose self-image, her verbal abuse, and constant berating took away my confidence. She wore me down. I was never allowed to give my opinion, and it seemed better to agree with her than to deal with her wrath and hysteria.

On every level, I didn't measure up. I was inadequate. Inferior. Undone.

My counselor explained very gently, "When your mother abandoned you emotionally, it was like a person throwing a baby into a swimming pool and yelling, 'Swim!'" That apt analogy resonated with me. I sometimes had felt as if I were drowning—in sorrow.

What caused my mother to self-destruct? Did she choose of her own volition to reject her responsibilities? Maybe she was punishing her husband. Or was she helpless, with no control over her actions? Was she paranoid schizophrenic, as the doctor suggested, or was her illness more sinister, resulting from her involvement in the occult? So many unanswered questions. Whatever the reason, she pulled the blinds down over my life.

"Dear Mommy"

Over the week, the counselor helped me see the cause of my depression. "As a child, your basic emotional needs were not met. You may have felt that you were not worth anything, which led you to feel angry. Since you were not allowed to direct your anger toward your mother, your anger turned inward. As depression.

"Your depression probably began years ago when you were a little girl, when you were too young to fend for yourself. And you've carried this burden of being estranged from your mother all these years. You've been running so fast, there was no time to soothe that wounded little girl down inside. She is hurt and angry, and she is still mourning her lost childhood and her mother."

"But what can I do?" I asked.

"I'm giving you an assignment," he said. "Tonight, I want you to write your mother a letter. Tell her all the hurt that you feel." He looked steadily at me. Then my kind, soft-spoken counselor said sternly, "I think you should tell her to go to hell!"

I was aghast. "I can't do that," I protested. "I could never do that. Besides, if I blame her for what she did to me, and she really couldn't help it, what's the use of being angry?" But he was adamant that I express my anger to her.

That night, I wrote a long letter. I poured out my heart. I told her how hard it was to be alone all those years and how lonely I felt. "You didn't prepare me for life!" I wrote. "You abandoned me when I needed you!" But I could not tell her to go to hell.

The counselor said my letter was a good *first step*! There was more to deal with, to dredge up, for sure, but for now I could function. Talking it out helped my heart to heal. I had revealed the secrets of my past and talked it out with a trusted counselor. Some of the layers had peeled off.

I drove back home to Miami, marveling at all the counselor had said.

Over the years, many other counseling sessions have helped me face the hurt of my past. I learned that whatever a child suffers, whether greatly or not so much, has a direct impact on his or her life as an adult.

Since everyone has struggles of some kind in childhood, overcoming is the name of the game.

My emotional pain through the years had been much heavier to bear than any physical pain. I was now ready to deal with the cancer, not fear it. Since the number of my days are in God's hands, I told myself, "Live in the moment, and don't worry about the future."

The years have passed, and I'm still here—at least, today. My Savior has the plan for my life. That assurance puts my mind at ease.

I never mailed the letter to my mother. It wasn't for her benefit; it was for mine. What was done could never be undone, but there could be healing in my heart if I forgave her. I wanted to. I knew I hadn't been such a great child either. I was headstrong and ungrateful. She had reminded me of that many times, and it was true. At times, I wished she would die, and then I'd be consumed with guilt at such a horrid thought.

But God had forgiven me of all I had ever done, so how could I not forgive her? And if she were truly helpless, how could I blame her?

I learned that a paranoid schizophrenic person may not have the emotional capacity to love. Did my mother ever love me? I think she did when I was little. But then she lost touch with reality and couldn't find her way back. I couldn't blame her for that.

Looking back, I realize that my life was quite an emotional journey, traveling down the tracks of my childhood, around the bend to adulthood, to arrive now, free of depression. Those memories that haunted me, that pulled me down, have lost their power. I can now hear the mournful wail of a train in the night and not feel dread. When a breeze wafts the scent of peonies and roses, carrying me back in time, I don't feel despair. My box of memories opens for a moment, and I feel sadness—but only for a moment. The old sorrow is now replaced with truth and contentment—and happiness.

I forgave her.

Final Meeting

The call came two days before Christmas in 1995, from a friend in Mansfield. With compassion, she gave me the news: "Your mother just died."

I cried a little when I heard the news, and then I didn't feel anything. It was absolutely weird. I called my friend Jeanne and told her I wasn't grieving. But then I added, "Actually, I've been in mourning for her for thirty-five years."

Jeanne said gently, "That's too long." All evening, those words rang in my head. *"That's too long."*

I wanted to see my mother one last time. She had not allowed me to see her all those years in real life, but she couldn't prevent me from going to her funeral.

Michelle and Laura were both home for the Christmas holidays, and they wanted to go with me. We flew to Columbus on Christmas Day. The funeral was the next day, on a bleak, cold Ohio morning, with snow flurries blowing. Everything was white—the sky, the snow, the ground. The landscape matched my mood.

Two of my dear friends from high school were waiting at the funeral home to welcome us. I hadn't seen them in years, and my emotions were raw. As we entered the viewing room, a couple standing by the casket saw us and immediately came over to us. They introduced themselves as my mother's third husband's nephew, Jim, and his wife, Viola. We talked for a moment, and I thanked them for taking care of my mother. Then Viola asked me, "What happened between you and your mother?"

Her blunt question jarred me. What should I say to this stranger? She probably had heard my mother's version many times. I decided to be blunt too. Put the truth out there and let the chips fall.

"She didn't want me to ever leave her, even for college or to get married," I said, "and when I did, she never forgave me." I paused and added, "And I became a follower of Jesus, and that made her furious."

Jim and Viola both looked shocked. Viola said, "Oh, that's so strange! She's been talking about going to heaven to be with Jesus!"

Now I was the one who was shocked. "My mother? Talking about Jesus?"

They both looked stunned and offended. The conversation wasn't going well. I felt irritated.

We excused ourselves, and my girls and I went up to the casket. As I looked down, I felt as if I were in a bad dream. It was a stranger who lay there in the casket. Not having seen her in thirty-five years, I never would have known this was my mother—this gray little woman who looked peaceful, even pretty. I felt no emotion. Nothing. I had loved her in my childhood, and I loved her still. But she had put me out to dry, to swing in the wind when I was too young. My wounds were so deep that I felt shut down.

Jim had arranged a service of sorts. He had not consulted with me, though legally I was the next of kin. My girls and I sat on the front row, waiting for the service to begin. I was amazed when a crowd began filling in the seats. There may have been sixty people there. My mother was a recluse—how did she know all these people?

Jim and his family, his six children and eleven grandchildren, huddled around the casket. Some of them were sobbing. One of Viola's daughters came over to us and gushed, "We loved your mother so much!" I just looked at her. I felt very confused. Another woman came up and said, "Your mother was such a blessing." I couldn't answer. Her words didn't compute in my brain.

Clearly, all of them were mourning. They missed her. They had a relationship with her. They loved her. How could that be?

My mind flashed back to when Michelle, then a junior in college, had gone to Ohio to try to visit my mother. She went to her house and knocked on the door. She heard a voice from inside: "Who is it?"

"I'm your granddaughter," Michelle called out.

The voice inside growled, "I'm busy!" She didn't open the door. She had broken Michelle's heart. And yet, she evidently embraced these people. How could she have cared for these strangers and not her precious granddaughters and me?

I felt an intense anger welling up. This scene was like something from *The Twilight Zone*. My girls were looking at me questioningly. I found out later that Laura had gone out to ask the funeral director if we were in the right room! Years later, she said, "But I never doubted you, Mom."

Certainly, I was doubting me. I didn't know what was really true. I was caught up in the same feelings I had felt as a child, when my mother talked at me, making no sense—the sensation one feels when trying to keep balanced on the shifting boards in a funhouse. I was off balance, grasping for air, trying to stay upright.

Maybe I am the one at fault, I thought. *Maybe I made the whole thing up!* I was distraught, and my emotions were wearing me out.

Somehow, I made it through the service. Afterward, we drove through the snow to the cemetery and then back to my mother's house, where Jim gave me a photo of my mother—a most awkward moment. (Many months later, Jim's lawyer sent me a check for a hundred dollars, my inheritance, the minimum requirement under the law.)

Before we left Ohio, I needed to see my old, dear friend Mary for consolation. She welcomed the three of us to her home with open arms. Her darling daughters, Pam and Barb, lightened the atmosphere, but I still felt unnerved.

I told them the details of the funeral, and they were astounded to hear about my mother's "other family." As we were leaving, Mary announced, "Wait! You have to see Duffy. My sweet dog, Duffy, died last week. And since the weather has been so cold, we put Duffy on the back porch."

With trepidation, I peeked out the back door. There was Duffy, "lying in state" like Stalin in Red Square. He was perfectly preserved in the freezing cold. I thought, *My mind is frozen too. This is the second dead body I've seen today.* We drove away wondering if this day could be any more bizarre.

But there was one more stop we had to make before the day was done. I wanted to see Mrs. Burgener, my next-door neighbor all my growing-up years. Thankfully, she was still alive. She was now a little old lady, living in a different neighborhood, but as sharp and sweet as ever. We showed up at her house, and she warmly invited us in. The four of us sat in her living room, and I marveled that we could be having this moment together. I told her we were in town for my mother's funeral.

"Mrs. Burgener, could you please tell me—tell us—about my life next door to you when I was a child? Tell us everything, anything, whatever you remember."

"Well, I remember you wandered around my backyard a lot. You picked up walnuts from my black walnut tree and asked me to crack them, so you could make a black walnut cake." I reminded her that she sometimes invited me into her kitchen for cookies and milk. Did she ever wonder what was happening in my house? But like a good neighbor, she never asked.

"What about my mother, Mrs. Burgener?" I persisted. "The main thing I want to know—is it true that my mother went to bed and stayed there for six years? Did you ever see her during those years?"

"I'll tell you about my relationship with your mother," she answered. "When you were quite young, your mother and I were friends, sort of. She invited me over to your house a couple of times to smoke marijuana! I believe you were in the second grade."

Well, this was shocking news! My mother smoking marijuana? And Mrs. Burgener too? I could hardly believe it.

"Then, the next year," Mrs. Burgener continued, "well, I never saw her after that. Sometimes I saw your father going to work, and of course, I saw you going to school, but I never saw your mother for about six years. Not once. But I *heard* her! In the summertime, when our windows were open, I could hear her yelling from her bedroom. She yelled all day long for you—giving you orders, telling you all the jobs she wanted you to do."

Our two houses were close together. My mother's upstairs bedroom window was opposite Mrs. Burgener's downstairs kitchen window. In the 1940s, no one I knew had air conditioning. In the summer, everyone's windows were open wide to catch any breeze. So, of course she could hear everything my mother yelled.

"I didn't see your mother all those years—not until she started leaving the house in the mornings to go to work. I think you were about fifteen by then. But your mother and I never spoke to each other. She wasn't interested in being friends with me then."

As she told about those years of my childhood, I wished we could have listened for hours, but the day was fading, and we had a long drive to Columbus to catch our plane. This time of being together, face to face with my dear neighbor, had been an affirmation for me. I felt jubilant. Mrs. Burgener had vindicated my memory and given me great relief. Her words were the strongest verification. Laura and Michelle heard her answers, and I felt very thankful that she was there to tell the story. My life as I remembered it was true. I hadn't made it up or embellished it—it was all true. For some reason, I felt great satisfaction and freedom. The truth had set me free.

When we returned home and I told Charlie about all the people crying at the funeral, he was as confused as I was. But I think now, without a doubt, their tears were real. I was grateful that someone had taken care of my mother's needs. Her new family had to be God's provision for her.

As I look back on all that happened, I'm not sure I would change any of it, even if I could. I am not mourning my lost childhood anymore. The past is past. God knew how my life would turn out. He is the one who set me free. The Lord redeemed me from my past and gave me a new life and a new family, and it has been quite a ride!

Jeremiah, the prophet, put it in perspective a long time ago: "'For I know the plans I have for you,' declares the Lord, 'plans to prosper you and not to harm you, plans to give you hope and a future'" (Jeremiah 29:11).

CHAPTER 13

—— ⚘ ——

Glory Years

AT OUR LAST holiday dinner together, I was overwhelmed with gratitude to God for answering the longing of my heart—a family. As I was carrying the dessert of apple crisp out to the patio, I *saw* the picture. There at the big table sat my wonderful daughters, my sterling sons-in-law, and the six adorable grandchildren. It was the picture in my mind of long ago—that spectacular Norman Rockwell painting of a family at a holiday feast, the picture of a family who loved each other.

I had dreamed of it, and here it was. It wasn't perfect, because there is no perfection here on this earth. When we all get together, we see each other's flaws. My blunders are the worst of all. I still act on impulse. I still get uptight, say too much, cause hurt feelings. The barriers rise up, and then I have to ask *again*, "Will you forgive me?" Thankfully, they do. And then we start over.

I love this challenge called life. Along the way, I've discovered a few things that I know to be true. I've observed that even our best and highest intentions don't completely satisfy. Getting married or raising children doesn't completely fulfill a person. Your status doesn't define you. Having a career does not produce peace. Neither prestige nor power brings purpose. Money can't make a happy atmosphere at the breakfast table.

What is the purpose of it all? I believe a person is just spinning her wheels until she is fulfilled by the ultimate: God Himself—Messiah Jesus.

He is the only one who can make a person complete, and He offers abundant and eternal life to all who put their trust in Him.

I know this from personal experience. As I grew up, my life was empty and filled with pain. As a baby, I was abandoned by my father; as a young girl, abandoned by my mother; and as a young woman, left alone to fend for myself. Three strikes—but not out.

God had the plan. He was there all along, and at the right time, He let me find Him. His blessings in my life could fill a thousand books. And the best is yet to come.

Someday, Jesus is coming back to make everything right. When He came the first time, He changed history, even the way we date our calendar. Jesus promised, "I am going to prepare a place for you and…I will come back and take you to be with Me…." A glorious Happy Ending. Or *Beginning*.

So now this ends my memoir—but it's not the end. I am looking forward to what lies ahead, and what a future that will be! I can't wait to see what God has prepared for us. When He calls my name, I will go to be with Him in heaven. There at last, I will live my *happily ever after*.

Made in the USA
Lexington, KY
20 November 2019

57366180R00081